The Art of Crème Brûlée

In The Art of Crème Brûlée, Chef Tran unveils over 50 wonderful recipes along with photographed techniques to create a smooth and tasty Crème Brûlée. Whether you are a beginner or a professional chef, each recipe will bring pleasure to your guests.

The Art of Crème Brûlée includes a brief history, techniques, equipment, and ingredients which can be found at any grocery or specialty store. All recipes are alphabetized for your convenience. The recipes are divided into two categories: small quantities for home use and large quantities for restaurant use.

the art of
Crème Brûlée

by Cam Tran
Chef de Pâtissier

Edited by Christine Mazur
& Michael Tran
Photography by Nik Travisone

Published by Blurb Books Inc
(www.blurb.com)
San Francisco, USA
London, UK

Copyright © Cam Tran 2018

All rights reserved. No part of this publication may be reproduced, stored in a retrieval system or transmitted in any form or by any means, electronic, mechanical, photocopying, recording or otherwise, without the prior permission of the copyright holder.

Printed in
United States
Canada
Netherlands

Acknowledgements
Editor: Christine Mazur & Andrew Toews
Final Editor: Michael Tran
Photographer: Nik Travisone

Notes on measurements:

All recipes contain metric and imperial measurements/weight followed by US/Canada cup conversions for relevant ingredients. All recipes are weighed or measured, tablespoons are assumed to be 15 millilitres (ml), 1 cup is assumed to be 250 ml and 1 oz is assumed to be 30 grams. Unless otherwise stated, milk is assumed to be full fat, heavy cream is 33 percent fat, and eggs are standard size three (large count). The yield in the recipes vary, depending on the weight of the eggs, measurements, and techniques.

ACKNOWLEDGEMENTS

To my friends Christine Mazur, Nik Travisone, Andrew Toews, and my brother Michael, without whom this book would have not been possible. My sincere thanks to Christine for understanding me in how I express my thoughts and putting up with all the grammatical errors. To Nik Travisone, for taking the pictures and fixing all my graphs. To my brother Michael, for putting in the time and effort in helping me complete this book.

CONTENTS

Introduction	12
Materials	15
Ingredients	20
Techniques	39
Recipes	53
Index	117
References	122

Preface

Writing a cookbook can be simple, but writing a cookbook with information about the many ingredients involved in the recipes can be very difficult. This book has taken me close to four years to complete. I do not want people to just follow my recipes, but to also understand the concept of making Crème Brûlée and learn the history and facts about the ingredients. My hope is that people can create their own Crème Brûlée and allow their imagination to grow. The information in this book was gathered from many sources. I would like to sincerely thank and give all the authors credit for their work. Without their information, and without the help of my friends, this book would have never been possible.

Introduction

Crème Brûlée is a rich and smooth-textured dessert made from a custard of egg yolks and heavy cream. Normally it is served cold with a hard caramel glaze covering the custard which shatters delightfully with the strike of a spoon. Crème Brûlée (pronounced "krem broo-ley") is derived from two French words meaning "burnt cream", which implies that the custard is made from cream that is burnt. The fact that neither the cream nor sugar crust are burnt suggests that the word "brûlée" was employed by mistake. Traditionally, a small round iron called a "salamander" was heated and then placed on top to caramelize the sugar—burning the cream and sugar instead of caramelizing them, hence the name "brûlée."

Today the world assumes that Crème Brûlée is French due to its name but, in fact, we do not know the exact origin of the dish. The earliest known reference to Crème Brûlée appeared in France in 1691, in François Massialot's cookbook, *Nouveau Cuisinier Royal et Bourgeois*.[1] The French name was later used in English translated books. In 1740, Massialot's *Nouveau Cuisinier* used the name "Crème à l'Angloise" to describe a similar recipe, but the dish was not seen again in French cookbooks until the 1980s.[2]

Meanwhile in England, the dish is known as "burnt cream" where it became popular in the 17th century. Legend has it that the dish was invented at Trinity College in Cambridge, 1879. According to Trinity College, however, there is no proof of this; since the late 19th century, a comparable dish known as Cambridge Burnt Cream or Trinity Cream has appeared in recipe books and is still served today in the kitchens of Trinity College.[3] Generally speaking, the British deny that Trinity Burnt Cream and Crème Brûlée are related.[4] While the French version is very sweet, British Trinity Cream is unsweetened and the topping is thicker and crustier.

The Spanish claim that they invented Crème Brûlée—which they call "Crema Catalana" or "Crema de Sant Josep"—in the 18th century, and that it is the true predecessor of what the dessert is today (100 years after the British claim the custard).[5] The difference between Crema Catalana and Crème Brûlée is that the latter is baked in a "bain marie," a shallow pan of water. Crema Catalana was traditionally served on March 19th, St. Joseph's Day, the equivalent of Father's Day.

As mentioned, while the dessert was called "burnt cream" in early 18th century England, the French term Crème Brûlée became popular in England only in the late 19th century. During this time, the recipe became more popular in France than anywhere else in the world. Crème Brûlée became the standard dessert in France and is offered in nearly every French restaurant.

Today, Crème Brûlée has become a standard dish in many American and Canadian restaurants. It is typically cooked in a small, round, and often white ceramic dish known as a ramekin. Some chefs may also use other small baking dishes that give a beautiful presentation and are attractive to the patrons' eyes. Generally, these dishes are shallow and small, and allow for even, consistent cooking of the cream resulting in a smooth texture and individually portioned for guests.

The modern day brûlée with its caramel crust can be achieved in many ways. The old fashioned crust-making method involved using a round heated iron applied directly to the top coating of sugar to melt it, but the heated iron is no longer feasible today. As previously mentioned, one method used by chefs is sprinkling the custard with sugar and broiling it under a "salamander," a special piece of kitchen equipment that creates high-intensity heat, melting the sugar to a caramelized state. This technique can be accomplished at home with a typical toaster oven using the broiler stage. A standard method typically used by the French to caramelize the sugar is a blowtorch. No matter which method, Crème Brûlée is not Crème Brûlée without the cream and a crust of caramelized sugar on top.

Materials

Before you begin making Crème Brûlée, make sure you have all the necessary equipment. Most items can be found in your kitchen. If you need to buy anything, it is worthwhile investing your money in good quality products that will last many years. Most of the tools needed to make Crème Brûlée can be found at any large department store or specialty kitchenware shop.

One item that might not be found at such places is a 9" x 6" x 4" stainless steel container with a lid used as a "Bain Marie" (see page 43). Specialized equipment like this may have to be purchased at a restaurant supplier or through the internet. However, the "Bain Marie" container is not essential as I will explain further in the "Technique" chapter.

The seven basic pieces of cooking equipment necessary to make Crème Brûlée are:

1. Whisk
2. Bowl
3. Measuring cup
4. Scales
5. Ramekins or other shallow ceramic bowls
6. Baking sheet
7. Blow torch or toaster oven

Whisk

Whisks come in many sizes and colours and are made from different materials—from plastic to stainless steel. A whisk allows you to combine ingredients together or break them apart. A whisk should be sturdy, not flimsy, and have a balloon shape.

Bowls

Bowls are made in many different sizes, materials, and shapes. Stainless steel bowls with a round base are the best choices, being sturdy and less likely to break compared to plastic. The round base allows you to combine every ingredient together compared to the hard-to-reach places of square-based bowls. Always use the right-sized bowl for the right amount of batter (for example, 250 ml of liquid in a 2 litre bowl).

Weighing and Measuring Tools

There are many different types of weighing system scales. Traditional balance scales are accurate and reliable, but are very time consuming. Traditional balance scales require weights and knowledge of mathematics. The weights are placed on one part of the scales, and the product used is added to the other part until it balances out with the weights.

Today the most common scales are digital and do not require weights or the use of math. After measuring the weight of each ingredient, digital scales can be tared or zeroed and the weight of the next ingredient can be added to the scale in use. It is worth investing money in a good quality product such as a scale that measures weights at 0.5 gram intervals to achieve accurate measurements and consistent results.

Measuring cups and spoons come in standard imperial and metric system measurements, and are only to be used for liquids, never solids. Pastry chefs in France are taught that one cup of sugar or flour always measures differently from one person to another; therefore, spices and other solids should only be weighed and not measured. If taste and appearance are not important to you, then measure away. Liquids should be measured by volume.

Ramekins or Ceramic Bowls

Ramekins are small, round, and shallow ceramic bowls typically used for making Crème Brûlée. A typical size is 3 inches in diameter with a 2 inch height. Small-sized ramekins are perfect for individual portions. Any ceramic dishes can be used, although they must be oven safe. Always use shallow dishes to ensure that the cream is evenly cooked which will achieve a smooth texture.

Baking Sheets

Aluminum, stainless steel, or Teflon baking sheets are acceptable so long as they are good quality products that will last a lifetime. Baking sheets allow ramekins to sit on an even surface while baking and prevents the brûlée from tipping over.

Blow Torch or Toaster Oven

Crème Brûlée is not Crème Brûlée without the brûlée—the burnt sugar crust on top. The most important equipment for achieving the burn is either a blow torch or a toaster oven. The blow torch burns the sugar with an intense heat, giving it a glass-like look when it hardens. There are two parts to the blow torch: the neck, which connects to the butane or propane tank; and the body, which is the tank itself. If you are not comfortable working with a blow torch, a toaster oven will also work.

Every toaster oven should have a broil setting to give intense heat at the top. This heat will burn or melt the sugar enough to achieve the desired glass appearance. Be forewarned, however, that a toaster oven usually takes longer to burn or melt the sugar while heating the whole dish, whereas the blow torch only heats the top. Therefore, when using a toaster oven, it is necessary to cool down the brûlée before serving it.

Other Equipment

Other equipment used in making Crème Brûlée can be found in your home: a rubber spatula for getting the last drop of mixture from the bowl, a ladle for pouring the Crème Brulée mixture into the ramekin dishes before baking, and string or elastic bands and cheese cloths for infusing flavour into the Crème Brulée mixture.

Ingredients

There are four major ingredients in Crème Brulée: cream, milk, sugar, and eggs. This section will explain each ingredient in detail including the process, uses, and history.

Cream

Cream[6] produced by cows often contain natural carotenoid pigments derived from the plants the animals eat. These pigments create the natural, slightly yellow tone, hence the name "cream." Cream is a dairy product composed of 3-66% fat known as milk fat or butter fat, the fat layer skimmed from the top of milk before homogenization. In non-homogenized milk, the fat rises to the surface. A centrifuge separator is used to spin the milk. Cream is then driven to the centre, leaving the milk behind. Cream is sold in pasteurized and ultra-pasteurized forms.

Pasteurization is the process of heating liquid foods to a specific temperature for a certain length of time: 160°F (71°C) for 15 seconds. Pasteurization is not intended to kill micro-organisms, but to reduce the viable pathogens while extending the shelf life of the product from spoilage. Ultra-pasteurization is when liquid foods are heated at a higher temperature: 166°F (74°C) for 30 seconds. Ultra-pasteurized products have a longer shelf life than pasteurized products due to the larger percentage of bacteria eliminated during the process.

Pasteurized and ultra-pasteurized products of milk and cream have no nutritional differences. Pure ultra-pasteurized products, however, do not whip well and may contain vegetable gums to compensate in order to make them more whippable.

**After thoroughly researching cream, I chose to create these charts primarily using information from the UK because it was more comprehensive. However, the percentage of milk fat and main uses are very similar for every country. Every country will have its own regulations.[7]

Cream varieties	% of milk fat	Main uses
Clotted cream	55%	Heat treated. Served as-is. A traditional part of English cream tea.
Extra-Thick Double cream	48%	Heat treated, then quickly cooled. Thick, fresh cream, used in pies, pudding and desserts (too thick to be poured).
Double cream	48%	Whips easily and can be piped when whipped.
Whipping cream	35%	Whips well, excellent for rich coffee creamer.
Whipped cream	35%	Already whipped. Used for decorations on cakes, pies, topping for ice cream, fruits etc.
Sterilized cream	23%	Sterilized. Used as coffee cream.
Cream or single cream	18%	Not sterilized. Used as coffee cream.
Sterilized half cream	12%	Sterilized. Commonly used as coffee cream.
Half cream	12%	Not sterilized. Commonly used as coffee cream.

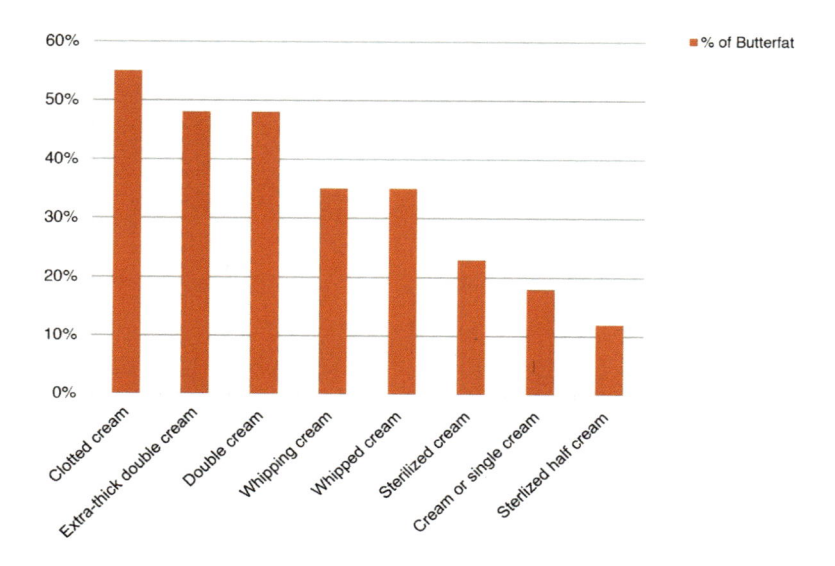

Milk

Milk[8] is a complicated product. It is a whitish liquid produced by the mammary glands of mammals. Milk is extracted from mammals during or after pregnancy. It is the primary source of nutrition for infant mammals before digestion of other foods. Milk is divided into two categories of consumption: a natural source of nutrition for infant mammals through breastfeeding, and a food product for consumption by humans.

Milk is processed into many varieties of dairy products such as cream, yogurt, butter, ice cream, and cheese. No one knows when the milk of animals was first used for human consumption, although it is believed to have first come into use around 10,000 BC when nomadic human tribes began settling into communities and raising domestic animals.

In Egypt, milk was a product prized by kings, priests, and the very wealthy. In Europe, 5th century AD, cows and sheep were valued for their milk. By the 14th century, cows' milk became more popular than sheeps' milk. European cows were being shipped to North America for their milk in the 17th century.

In 1862, the revolution of milk safety occurred with Louis Pasteur's great discovery of pasteurisation. When I lived in France, milk was never refrigerated, having been Ultra Heat Treatment (UHT) pasteurised. In this process milk is heated to a very high temperature (above 275°F (135°C) - 284°F (140°C)) for 2 to 6 seconds. The drawback of UHT is that it can cause Maillard browning (a chemical reaction between amino acids and reducing sugar), and slightly bitter and scalded flavours. The benefit of UHT milk is that it has a shelf life of six to nine months unrefrigerated.

Cattle produces about 85 percent of the world's milk supply. There are about 142 million dairy cows throughout the world that produce about 500,000 metric tons of milk each year.[9] The world consumes an average of 182,000 metric tons of fluid milk per year, and the rest is produced into other dairy products like cheese.[10] Canadians consume an average of 71 litres of milk per year, per person.[11]

Milk is considered to be essential to a daily balanced diet. It is one of the most important food groups providing nearly all the nutrients humans need for growth and good health: water, carbohydrates, fat, proteins, minerals, and vitamins.

Water — our bodies consist of 60% water which is essential to carry out all of its life processes.[12]

Carbohydrates — major source of energy for the body. Lactose in milk helps the body absorb minerals like calcium and phosphorus.

Fat — provides energy and essential fatty acids that the body needs.

Proteins — also supplies energy. Proteins help the body grow, building blood and tissue.

Minerals — helps the body grow and remain healthy. An important mineral is calcium. It is the essential source in bone structure and healthy teeth. One cup of low-fat milk contains about 300 mg of calcium. A daily intake of two cups of low-fat milk (600 mg) is recommended for adults and children, whereas 3 cups is recommended for teenagers.[13]

Vitamins — essential for growth, maintaining body tissue, and prevention of disease. Milk is an excellent source of vitamins A and B12.

Milk composition analysis, 100 grams					
Constituents	Unit	Cow	Goat	Sheep	Water buffalo
Water	g	87.8	88.9	83	81.1
Protein	g	3.2	3.1	5.4	4.5
Fat	g	3.9	3.5	6	8
Saturated fatty acids	g	2.4	2.3	3.8	4.2
Monounsaturated fatty acids	g	1.1	0.8	1.5	1.7
Polyunsaturated fatty acids	g	0.1	0.1	0.3	0.2
Carbohydrate	g	4.8	4.4	5.1	4.9
Cholesterol	mg	14	10	11	8
Calcium	mg	120	100	170	195
Energy	kcal	66	60	95	110
	kJ	275	253	396	463

[14]

Milk is available in many forms.[15]

- Whole milk contains 3.25 % fat
- Skim milk has virtually all fat removed from whole milk
- 2% milk contains 2% fat
- 1% milk contains 1% fat
- Dried milk is whole milk that has 95-98% of the water removed.
- Fortified milks are added with vitamins A and D.
- Acidophilus milk is a milk with added bacteria (lactobacillus acidophilus).
- Evaporated milk is whole milk with half of its water content removed.
- Condensed milk is whole milk that has sugar added and half of the water removed.
- Buttermilk is the residue left from the butter-making process using heavy cream.

Milk and other dairy products provide many health benefits. Milk helps the body develop, prevents osteoporosis, cavities, and chronic bronchitis. Skim milk is lower in cholesterol and prevents high blood pressure. Acidophilus milk products have nutritional value for colon cancer patients.

Many people cannot drink milk because they lack sufficient levels of lactase, the enzyme that breaks down the milk sugar lactose. Lactose intolerance, a condition which makes it difficult to digest milk, is prevalent in many ethnic groups and an estimated 60% of people develop lactose intolerance to some degree.

Photography by Cam Tran

Sugar

Sugar is classified as a sweet-flavoured substance used as food and found in the tissues of most plants.[16] A complex substance that we consume daily, sugar is a sucrose consisting of carbohydrates naturally present in fruits and vegetables. Carbohydrates are composed of three elements: carbon, hydrogen, and oxygen.

All green plants manufacture sugar through photosynthesis, the process by which plants convert sunlight into their food and energy supply. Once photosynthesis creates sugar, plants have the unique ability to change that sugar to starch, and from starch to various other sugars for storage. This diversity provides us with a wide variety of tasty fruits and vegetables, from the banana to the potato.

Sugars are present in sugar beets and sugarcane in higher concentrations than in any other plants. Sugarcane contains 12-14 percent sugar and sugar beets contain 16-18 percent. Sugarcane is a giant perennial grass, mostly cultivated in tropical or subtropical climates, especially in Asia.

In the 18th century, sugar plantations expanded from Asia into the West Indies and the Americas. This was the first time that sugar became available to the common people who previously relied on honey to sweeten foods.

Sugar beet is a root crop that is cultivated in cooler climates, and it became a major source of sugar in the 19th century. According to the USDA World Sugar Market and Trade Report, the world produced approximately 170 million tonnes of sugar in 2014.[17] The average person consumes about 20 kilograms of sugar per year.[18]

Various types of sugar are derived from different sources. Simple sugars are monosaccharides which include glucose, fructose, and galactose. Table or granulated sugar, which is most commonly used as food, is a disaccharide. Other disaccharides include maltose and lactose.

Sugar extraction

Sugar extraction is a very complicated process, but here is a simplified description. The sugarcane is washed and cleaned to remove the impurities. The cane goes through a milling plant where it is ground and pressed to extract the juice. Sugarcane juice is boiled, removing the water until it thickens and begins to crystallize, a method called "multiple-effect evaporation." The crystallized sugars are then spun in a centrifuge, removing the remaining liquid producing raw sugar (also known as damp sugar). The damp sugar crystals are then dried in a granulator. The dried sugar crystals are sorted, packaged, and shipped.

Sugar Varieties

Sugar varieties

Sugar varieties	Definitions	Uses
Granulated sugars	Commonly known as table, or white sugar. The colour is stripped, filtered and recrystallized from raw sugar. The grain size is about 0.5 mm across.	Commonly used in baking. Granulated sugars do not cake together, making them perfect for measuring or sprinkling onto food and drinks, especially coffee and tea.
Caster sugar	Fine granulated sugar. The grain size is about 0.35 mm. Castor or caster sugar is fine enough to fit though a "caster" or sprinkler.	Mostly used in delicate pastry or smooth desserts such as meringues, mousse, or pudding. Excellent for cold beverages where heat is not required to dissolve the sugar.
Confectioners or powdered sugar	Known as "icing sugar." Granulated sugar that has been finely ground and mixed with corn starch (around 4%) to prevent caking.	Commonly used in icing, glazes, filling, cake decorating and some pastries.
Brown sugar	Brown sugar is white sugars that is coated with molasses. Brown sugars is softer and moister than white. The light and dark sugar refers to amount of molasses present.	Light brown sugars is used in baking, sauces and glazes. Dark sugars are used in richer foods like gingerbread cookies.
Coarse or decorating sugar	Has a larger crystal than granulated sugar. Is stronger and more resistant to heat due to the large crystal size.	Mostly used for decorating cake. Gives baked goods or candies a little texture.
Inverted sugar	A liquid or paste made from a sucrose-water solution that is heated with an addition of acid. It does not crystalize, and retains moisture.	Mostly used in ice cream and sorbet where ice formation is prevented. Used in baked goods for moisture retention. Also used in glazes, sauces, fondant and candy making.
Demerara sugar	A raw sugar form that does not have all the molasses refined out. It comes from the first of three crystallization stages in the production of cane sugar. Grains are large and crunchy.	Used to dissolve in hot cereals, is sprinkled onto baked goods, perfect for tea and coffee.
Molasses	A dark liquid substance which is the byproduct (residue) of refined sugarcane, beets and grapes into granulated sugar. Comes from the third boiling stage of sugar syrup, and is the concentrated byproduct left over after the sugar's sucrose is crystallized. The darker the molasses, the more bitter it is.	Mostly added to recipes such as gingerbread cookies for flavour, colour, and moisture, but not for sweetness.
Honey	Sugar syrup made by bees from the nectar secreted from certain flowers.	Commonly used as a sweetener for teas. Most used in baking in liquid forms.

This information in this chart comes from many resources listed at the end of this book

Photography by Cam Tran

EGGS

Eggs are produced by the females of species like birds, reptiles, amphibians, and fish. Eaten by humans for thousands of years, eggs are one of the most nutritional and versatile foods we consume.[19] Eggs vary in size and colour depending on the species. Approximately 2.3 billion chicken eggs are consumed each year. Chicken eggs are one of North America's favourite breakfast foods. They are served in many ways including scrambled, fried, or poached, and are an essential ingredient for bakers and pastry chefs. As is taught at the Gastronomicom pastry school, a large chicken egg weighs 50 to 55 grams (g) with the yolk weighing approximately 20 g and egg whites about 30 g.[20] Eggs contain all the essential amino acids humans need, plus vitamins and minerals. They consist of three major components: shell, egg white, and yolk.

Shell — the hard exterior part of an egg. The shell is slightly porous and is made up of calcium carbonate. The porous nature of the shell allows it to absorb odours and flavours; therefore, it is essential to keep strong odorous foods away from eggs, if possible. Egg shells vary in colour depending on the type of species. Some egg shells like quail eggs have black and white spots while others are solid white like duck eggs. Chicken eggs come in two colours: either white or brown. The colour indicates the breed of hen, but has no connection with the quality or flavour of the eggs.

Albumen — This clear liquid commonly called egg white consists of 10% protein, 90% water, and small traces of vitamins. The primary purpose of the egg white is to protect the yolk and provide nutrition for the embryo. A large egg white weighs an average of 30 g, consisting of protein, carbohydrate, sodium, calories, and no cholesterols. Egg whites have many uses in foods such as meringue and clarifying soups, as well as in vaccines (such as those used for influenza).

Yolk — contains large amounts of protein and choline and is widely used in cookeries, especially pastry. A large egg yolk weighs an average of 20 g, consisting of protein, cholesterol, carbohydrates, and fat. Egg yolks contain vitamins A, D, E, K, iron, and thiamin. The yolk is located in the centre of the egg white and is surrounded by a colourless membrane. A little white spot, the "germinal disc," attaches to the yolk and is where fertilization takes place.

Nutritional Composition of One Large Egg (2 oz/56 g)

	Whole Egg	Egg White	Egg Yolk
Weight	56 g	38 g	17 g
Calories	84	20	64
Total fat	6 g	0 g	6 g
Monounsaturated fat	2.5 g	0 g	2.5 g
Polyunsaturated fat	0.7 g	0 g	0.7 g
Saturated fat	2	0 g	2 g
Cholesterol	213 mg	0 mg	213 mg
Sodium	71 mg	62 mg	9 mg
Carbohydrate	0.6 g	0.3 g	0.3 g
Dietary fiber	0 g	0 g	0 g
Sugar	0 g	0 g	0 g
Protein	6.6 g	3.9 g	2.7 g
Vitamin A	99 mcg	0 mcg	99 mcg
Vitamin C	0 mg	0 mg	0 mg

	Whole Egg	Egg White	Egg Yolk
Vitamin D	22 mg	0 mg	22 mg
Vitamin E	1.3 mg	0 mg	1.3 mg
Vitamin K	25 mg	0 mg	25 mg
Thiamin (B1)	0.4 mg	0 mg	0.4 mg
Riboflavin (B2)	0.26 mg	0.15 mg	0.11 mg
Pantothenic acid (B5)	0.74 mg	0.05 mg	0.69 mg
Pyridoxine (B6)	0.07 mg	0 mg	0.07 mg
Folate (B9)	25 mg	1 mg	24 mg
Calcium	27 mg	4 mg	23 mg
Iron	0.6 mg	0.01 mg	0.6 mg
Magnesium	6 mg	4 mg	2 mg
Phosphorus	87 mg	4 mg	83 mg
Potassium	63 mg	47 mg	16 mg
Zinc	0.53 mg	0.002 mg	0.53 mg
Choline	135 mg	0 mg	135 mg

[21]

Two twisted, whitish cords are located opposite each end of the yolk and are known as "chalazae." The function of the chalazae is to anchor the yolk in the centre of the egg white. Chalazae have no nutritional value and vary in size and density. The yolk varies in colour particularly in eggs from free-range chickens. Farmers are able to emphasize the colour of the yolks by providing hens with feeds of alfalfa and yellow corn which contain a fat-soluble pigment. The pigments in chicken feed determine the colour of the yolks from nearly white and yellow to orange and red. If the diet of hens contain capsicum (pepper plant), the result is orange to red yolks. If the diet of the hens contains yellow or orange plant pigments known as xanthophyll, the result is dark yellow or orange yolks. The colour of the yolks has no nutritional influence.

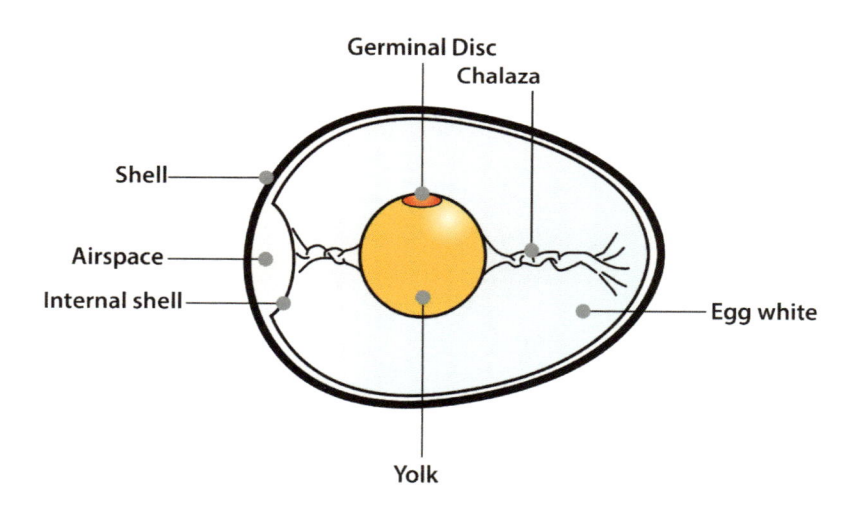

Diagram by Nik Travisione

Grading and Sizing — In Canada, eggs are graded, sized, and packed according to the standards of the Canadian Food Inspection Agency (CFIA). At the grading station, eggs are washed and sanitized in a high-speed washer. The eggs are examined over a bright light which makes the interior visible in a process called "candling." Under the light, any defects in the eggs become visible. Eggs failing to meet CFIA standards are removed. Based on CFIA criteria, eggs are divided into grades. The examiner grades the eggs according to the size of the airspace between the egg white and the shell (see diagram).

Size	Mass per gram
Jumbo	70 g or more
Extra Large	63 g – 69 g
Large	56 g – 62 g
Medium	49 g – 55 g
Small	42 g – 48 g
Peewee	Less than 41 g

The information from this chart is from several resources listed at the end of this book.

Eggs with a small airspace are graded as AA. As the airspace increases in volume, the grades move from AA to A to B, and the quality of the eggs decrease. They become less dense and with the increase of airspace volume, they eventually float in water at which point they should not be consumed. As eggs age, the egg white becomes watery when cooked. This is due to the egg white's chemical breakdown.

In Canada, Europe, and other countries, eggs are graded based on farming production. Eggs laid by free-range chickens and organic are typically higher in price than eggs from caged chickens.

Egg Chemistry[22]

Eggs play a major role in cooking and the baking process. Eggs have many purposes: it is a natural leavening agent, and acts as an emulsifier and binding agent. Understanding egg chemistry helps you understand their roles. Eggs contain proteins, carbohydrates, fats, and vitamins as mentioned. Egg proteins are important, as they tend to change when heated, whipped, or combined with other ingredients.

Egg white proteins are globular, which means the protein molecules are twisted, folded, and curled up in a spherical shape surrounded by water. Egg white proteins contain amino acids which play two roles: they either attract water (hydrophilic) or repel water (hydrophobic).

Hydrophobic amino acids are in the centre of the sphere and hydrophilic amino acids are on the outside of the sphere closer to the water.

Introducing air bubbles to egg proteins causes the proteins to uncurl so that hydrophilic amino acids are immersed in the water and the hydrophobic amino acids can bind to the air. As the proteins uncurl, multiple bonds are created with other unraveled proteins producing a network of flexible, elastic film that can hold air bubbles in place, thus becoming a foam. This process is called coagulation or binding. Meringues, angel food cake, soufflés, and sponge cakes are some examples of beaten egg whites that hold millions of air bubbles.

When the captured air bubbles are heated, they expand as the gas inside them is also heated. The elastic film surrounding the air bubbles solidifies and the structure is maintained after the bubbles burst. This example of a natural leavening agent is especially used in angel food cake. Overwhipping the egg whites causes the protein molecules to be overstretched. The molecules become weak and unstable, and this may cause the egg whites to collapse in the bowl or later in the oven. Overwhipped egg whites become clumpy, grainy, dry, and hard to fold into the batter.

Emulsion is a mixture of two or more liquids that are unmixable or unblendable. A vinaigrette is an example of oil-water emulsion. Egg yolks act as an emulsifier, and it has the ability to bind liquids and fats together, creating an emulsion that prevents them from separating. This is very important in the baking process of Crème Brûlée and other foods such as mayonnaise and hollandaise .

In Crème Brûlée, when egg yolks are heated, egg yolk proteins uncurl and bind to form a mesh that traps cream or milk in a soft gel. The emulsion process aids in even distribution of liquids and fats for a smooth batter and creamy custards. If too much heat is applied, the egg protein will gel too much and turn grainy and curdled.

Eggs can hold air bubbles, but are not as efficient compared to whipped egg whites for creating emulsion. Eggs are an excellent binding agent for cooking and baking especially in cakes, pastries, desserts, meat loaves, and breading. When eggs are heated, the egg proteins coagulate thus binding the ingredients together. The firming of egg proteins perform another function: it gives structural supports to delicate desserts and pastries.

TECHNIQUES

Secrets! Ah, the French do not like to share unless you are a qualified apprentice. This is the reason why French chefs are ranked among the best and why France is considered to be the birthplace of culinary arts. A chef's secret is passed down only to their apprentices.

After my graduation from Red River College, I worked under a French Canadian chef for four years. Making Crème Brûlée is very different today compared to 18 years ago. Every chefs' technique is different. As a trained pastry chef, I can attest to the fact that the technique of making Crème Brûlée is very specialized and that the French define a properly made Crème Brûlée by its creamy texture and caramelization of sugar.

Making the Crème Brûlée mixture is not complicated. Inexperienced chefs or cooks can make a decent product. The baking process can get a little complicated, but it is a matter of grasping a simple understanding of the chemistry process. There are two methods of baking Crème Brûlée which I will explain later. Let`s start with the basics!

Whisking

There are wrong ways to whisk which people do not realize. This starts with equipment ratio. For example, never use a big balloon (or three-inch) whisk for a small bowl (three inches wide) where air cannot be incorporated or mixtures cannot be properly beaten. The rule of thumb is that the bowl should be three to four times bigger than the whisk. The speed of whisking is important as well, especially when adding hot liquid cream to the egg mixture. If the whisking speed is slow, the egg will cook, creating grained size balls and will cause the Crème Brûlée to be lumpy. Another way of preventing lumps in the Crème Brûlée mixture is to immediately whisk the eggs and sugar together once they are combined. If egg and sugar are left unattended for a long period of time, the air will cause the egg yolks to dry out.

Infusion

Flavour, flavour, flavour! It`s what Crème Brûlée is all about. The flavours of Crème Brûlée are endless: it's about being creative and using your imagination. Do you ever wonder how different flavours of Crème Brûlée are made? It's a very simple technique: infusion. Infusion allows the flavour of the infusing ingredient (usually a strong scented flower or citrus skin) to be absorbed into the cream. Depending on the ingredient, infusion can take anywhere from 10 minutes to 12 hours.

Infusion should start with a hot liquid which allows for better absorption of flavour and increases the speed of infusion. To infuse an ingredient, you will require two items: cheese cloths and a string or elastic band. This allows loose ingredients to be kept within a cloth so that straining the ingredient out of the mixture after infusion is not required.

To infuse, put the ingredient in the middle of a 6 x 6 inch cheese cloth, bring all corners together like a bag, and tie them together with a string or elastic band. Bring the cream to a boil and place the cheese cloth bag right in the pot. Make sure the bag is fully absorbed by the cream by pushing it down, allowing the bag to be soaked. If the infusion time requires more than one hour, the cream has to be cooled down with an ice water bath (see page 42 for instructions).

After the appropriate amount of infusion time has passed, remove the cheese cloth and squeeze as much liquid out as possible. This allows the full flavour of the ingredients to be infused into the cream. After the infusion, re-measure the liquid. Liquid tends to be lost due to evaporation and can be absorbed by the cheese cloth and the infusing ingredients. After infusion, add more cream if necessary to balance the original measurement of liquids required by the recipe.

Ice Bath

Ice bath is a term used by all chefs and cooks that refers to a container filled with ice and water used to cool a product down to prevent bacteria growth.[23] When I studied culinary arts, students were taught that perishable food products can experience exponential bacteria growth in three hours—going from 1 bacterium to 512 in this amount of time.[24] The amount of bacteria growth can vary depending on the bacteria species. After adding the sachet to the cream for infusion, the cream will need to be cooled down immediately to reduce the growth of bacteria if the infusion requires more than one hour. To reduce the bacteria growth, put the pot of infused cream in a bowl or container filled with ice and water. The ice water should cover ¾ of the pot. Whisk or stir constantly while the pot of cream is in the ice bath. Once the infused cream is cold, cover the pot with a plastic film to prevent dirt or any other debris from falling in. Refrigerate and continue with the recipe instructions.

Baking

One of the most important factors of making Crème Brûlée is how it is baked. There are two methods of baking Crème Brûlée: direct heat and water bath. For many years, I have been using a water bath method known as "Bain Marie." This method was taught at Red River College and used by the French Canadian chef I worked under immediately after completing my studies.

The Bain Marie method requires a shallow stainless steel baking container and lid which is called an "insert pan." The insert pan should be approximately 9 x 6 x 4 inches deep. Other baking dishes can be used if the height, width, and depth are larger than the ramekins. The ramekins should fit inside with a little space between them, not snug. The insert pan can be found at any local specialty baking supplies store or restaurant equipment supplier.

The Bain Marie method uses heated water and steam, cooking the exterior of the ramekin and exposed liquid. This method has advantages and disadvantages.

The advantage of using the Bain Marie is that the baking time is shortened. The disadvantage is that the heat intensity of the steam cannot be controlled; therefore, there is a risk of overcooking the Crème Brûlée if it is not checked regularly, creating a undesired texture of scrambled eggs. When using the Bain Marie method, check the Crème Brûlée constantly during the baking process by opening the lid and observing the texture. The Crème Brûlée must be checked every five minutes while baking. Observe the mixture's texture and jiggle the ramekins if it's too hard to tell just by looking.

The Direct Heat method is one that I have been using since I graduated from the Gastronmicom pastry school in France. Again, there are advantages and disadvantages to this method. The advantage of using this method is the consistent cooking temperature. Cooking with direct heat results in perfectly smooth Crème Brulée without over-baking even if you leave it unattended for a short period which, however, I do not recommend.

As with the Bain Marie method, the Crème Brûlée must be checked every five minutes while baking. Observe the mixture's texture and jiggle the ramekins if it is too hard to tell just by looking. The oven temperature must be at 212°F (100°C). If it is more than that, the Crème Brûlée will bubble and the interior will be airy when cool, almost like the consistency of scrambled eggs. Before baking, note the air temperature of your kitchen. If it is too hot, lower the oven temperature by 41°F (5°C) - 50°F (10°C) or so to compensate for the extra heat that will otherwise cause it to over-bake (every residential or commercial oven is different, so adjust the temperature accordingly).

One disadvantage of the Direct Heat method is the time required for baking. If you are in a hurry, forget about this method. The time depends on the quantity that you are baking. For restaurants, cafés, or hotels, it takes roughly 20 minutes to one hour. For home use, the baking time ranges from 10 - 25 minutes. The other disadvantage to Direct Heat is that nothing else can be baked in that oven at the same time if higher temperatures are required; this is very important for chefs in a commercial kitchen where oven space is limited.

Step-by-Step Bain Marie Method

1) Preheat oven to 350°F (176°C).
2) Put ramekins or baking dishes in the insert pan.
3) Fill ramekins with Crème Brûlée mixture, liquid slightly below the rim.
4) Slowly pour hot water in the insert pan to ¾ of the ramekin height.
5) Cover the insert pan and bake approximately 10 minutes.
6) Check Crème Brûlée every 5 minutes to prevent overcooking. Observe the mixture's texture and jiggle the ramekins if it's too hard to tell just by looking.
7) Once the mixture is slightly solidified, remove ramekins from the water bath to prevent overcooking.
8) Allow ramekins to cool down at room temperature for 5 - 10 minutes, then place in the refrigerator. When the Crème Brûlée is cold, caramelize (i.e. melt) the sugar and serve.

Step-by-Step Direct Heat Method

1) Preheat oven to 212°F (100°C). Adjust to temperature of room as necessary.
2) Put ramekins on a baking sheet.
3) Fill ramekins with Crème Brûlée mixture to slightly below the rim.
4) Bake for approximately 10 - 25 minutes depending on batch size, checking every 5 minutes. Observe the mixture's texture and jiggle the ramekins if it's hard to tell just by looking.
5) Once the mixture is slightly solidified, remove the baking sheet from the oven.
6) Allow ramekins to cool down at room temperature for 5 - 10 minutes, then place in the refrigerator. When Crème Brûlée is cold, caramelize (i.e. melt) the sugar and serve.

Example of Direct Heat Method: Making White Chocolate Black Pepper Crème Brûlée

Step 1) Measure the cream and bring to a rolling boil.

Step 2) Pour hot cream over white chocolate.

Step 3) Whisk cream slowly until chocolate is melted.

Step 4) Weigh out eggs.

Step 5) Tare the scale. Weigh out sugar on top of the eggs.

Step 6) Whisk until thoroughly blended.

Step 7) Whisk the chocolate cream mixture into the egg mixture.

Step 8) Whisk the mixture until thoroughly blended.

Step 9) Weigh the black pepper.

Step 10) Pour in black pepper.

Step 11) Whisk until thoroughly blended.

Step 12) Pour or ladle the mixture into the ramekins.

Step 13) Use a blowtorch to remove the air bubbles.

49

Step 14) Place baking sheet in the oven and bake at 212°F (100°C) for approx 10 to 20 minutes as described above.

Step 15) When Brûlée is cold, sprinkle approximately 15 ml of sugar on top.

Step 16) Spread the sugar evenly.

Step 17) Caramelize (melt) the sugar with blow torch, passing the flame gently back and forth across the sugared top until it has just melted to a clear, hard appearance. This may take practice as sugar burns easily.

Ratio

Eggs are one of the major components in the process of making Crème Brûlée. Understanding the egg chemistry and infusion allows you to create your own recipes. When egg proteins are heated, it coagulates, binding the ingredients together. The coagulation or binding of the ingredients depends on three factors: the amount of egg protein to liquid, temperature, and time.

Egg yolk to cream ratio in Crème Brûlée is crucial. If the amount of cream or milk exceeds the egg yolk proteins that it can bind too, the coagulation and structural support needed will not occur. Therefore, we must follow a certain ratio. After my experimental test, the ratio of 20 g egg yolk protein can bind or coagulate with 80 - 140 ml of liquid cream that will give you a rich and smooth custard without a dry crust during baking. The coagulation time varies from 15 minutes to 45 minutes depending on the amount of liquid used; more liquid, more time. If the ratio of egg yolk to cream exceeds my recommendation, the Crème Brûlée will not be as rich and smooth, and the crust will be dry.

Sugar ratio depends on personal taste. People either like it sweet or not. My standard is 16 g of sugar to 100 ml of liquid. The sugar content in this book varies, and this depends on the ingredients infused or added to the cream. If the ingredients contain acids, then extra sugar will be required.

When following a recipe, you can always adjust the sugar content by adding less than the amount required or increase the amount to your personal taste buds. Note that you cannot take away sugar once added to a recipe and extra sugar will be required for the final stage of the Crème Brulée.

Recipes

** Please note, the original recipes are created for restaurant use in large quantities. I converted the recipes into smaller proportions for home use. A simple calculation is required for restaurant use. The yield amount will vary between 1 to 4 oz.

Almond and White Chocolate Crème Brûlée

125 g white chocolate (if using chocolate chunks, chop into small pieces)	500 g white chocolate (if using chocolate chunks, chop into small pieces)
25 g almond powder	100 g almond powder
200 ml whipping cream	800 ml whipping cream
350 ml soy almond milk	1400 ml soy almond milk
25 g sugar	100 g sugar
3 1/2 egg yolks (70 g)	14 egg yolks (280 g)
1 egg (56 - 62 g)	4 eggs (224 - 248 g)

Yield: 7 x 2 oz approx.   **Yield:** 28 x 2 oz approx.

1) Put chocolate chips or pieces in a mixing bowl and set it aside.
2) In a pot, bring cream and soy almond milk to a rolling boil. Remove from heat. Pour the hot cream over the chocolate. Whisk slowly until chocolate is melted and thoroughly blended. Set it aside.
3) In a mixing bowl, combine eggs (both yolks and egg(s)), sugar, and almond powder. Whisk until thoroughly blended.
4) Whisk the chocolate cream mixture into the egg mixture. Whisk until thoroughly blended.
5) Put ramekins on a baking sheet.
6) Fill ramekins with Crème Brûlée mixture, liquid slightly below the rim.
7) Bake using the Direct Heat method, checking every 5 minutes.
8) Once the mixture is slightly solidified, remove the baking sheet from the oven. Allow ramekins to cool down at room temperature for 5 - 10 minutes and refrigerate. When Brûlée is cold, caramelize (i.e. melt) the sugar and serve.

Avocado Crème Brûlée

42 g avocado
180 ml whipping cream
60 ml milk
41 g sugar
1 3/4 egg yolks (35 g)

210 g avocado
900 ml whipping cream
300 ml milk
205 g sugar
9 egg yolks (180 g)

Yield: 6 x 2 oz approx.

Yield: 30 x 2 oz approx.

1) In a food processor or blender, purée the avocado with milk until smooth. Set it aside.
2) In a pot, bring cream to a rolling boil. Remove from heat. Set it aside.
3) In a mixing bowl, combine egg yolks and sugar. Whisk until thoroughly blended.
4) Slowly pour and whisk the hot cream into the egg mixture. Whisk until thoroughly blended.
5) Whisk the avocado mixture into the cream mixture. Whisk until thoroughly blended.
6) Put ramekins on a baking sheet.
7) Fill ramekins with Crème Brûlée mixture, liquid slightly below the rim.
8) Bake using the Direct Heat method, checking every 5 minutes.
9) Once the mixture is slightly solidified, remove the baking sheet from the oven. Allow ramekins to cool down at room temperature for 5 - 10 minutes and refrigerate. When Brûlée is cold, caramelize (i.e. melt) the sugar and serve.

Banana and Passion Fruit Crème Brûlée

75 g banana	300 g banana
38 g frozen passion fruit purée or 75 g fresh passion fruit	150 g frozen passion fruit purée or 300 g fresh passion fruit
125 ml whipping cream	500 ml whipping cream
65 ml milk	250 ml milk
2 egg yolks (40 g)	8 egg yolks (160 g)
1/2 egg (28 g - 31 g)	2 eggs (112 - 124 g)
33 g sugar	130 g sugar

Yield: 7 x 2 oz approx.   **Yield:** 28 x 2 oz approx.

1) In a food processor or blender, purée the bananas with milk until smooth. Set it aside.
2) In a pot, bring cream and passion fruit purée to a rolling boil (if using fresh passion fruit, purée the fruits in a food processor or blender until liquid starts to form. Strain the liquid though a fine mesh, extracting the juice). Remove from heat. Set it aside.
3) In a mixing bowl, combine eggs (both yolks and egg(s)) and sugar. Whisk until thoroughly blended.
4) Slowly pour and whisk the hot cream mixture into the egg mixture. Whisk until thoroughly blended.
5) Whisk the banana mixture into the cream mixture. Whisk until thoroughly blended.
6) Put ramekins on a baking sheet.
7) Fill ramekins with Crème Brûlée mixture, liquid slightly below the rim.
8) Bake using the Direct Heat method, checking every 5 minutes.
9) Once the mixture is slightly solidified, remove the baking sheet from the oven. Allow ramekins to cool down at room temperature for 5 - 10 minutes and refrigerate. When Brûlée is cold, caramelize (i.e. melt) the sugar and serve.

Basil and Lemon Crème Brûlée

200 ml whipping cream	1000 ml whipping cream
66 ml milk	330 ml milk
7 g fresh basil	35 g fresh basil
10 g or 1/2 lemon zest	50 g or 3 lemon zest
6.4 g or 1/4 lemon, juiced	32 g or 1 lemon, juiced
34 g sugar	170 g sugar
1/2 egg (28 - 31 g)	2 eggs (112 - 124 g)
1 1/2 egg yolks (30 g)	8 egg yolks (160 g)

Yield: 7 x 2 oz approx.   **Yield:** 34 x 2 oz approx.

The recipe below is in small quantities. Please change the amount of cream and milk required for large quantities.

1) In a pot, bring 200 ml cream and 66 ml milk to a rolling boil. Remove from heat. Infuse the sachet of basil and lemon zest in the hot cream (see page 40 for infusion instructions). Cool the cream in an ice bath (see page 42 for ice bath instructions). Refrigerate and infuse for 2 hours.
2) After the infusion time, remove the sachet and squeeze as much liquid out as possible back into the cream.
3) In a measuring cup, re-measure the cream to 266 ml. Add cream if necessary to reach 266 ml.
4) In a pot, bring infused cream to a rolling boil. Remove from heat. Set it aside.
5) In a mixing bowl, combine eggs (both yolks and egg(s)) and sugar. Whisk until thoroughly blended.
6) Slowly pour and whisk the hot infused cream into the egg mixture. Whisk until thoroughly blended.
7) Whisk lemon juice into the cream mixture. Whisk until thoroughly blended.
8) Put ramekins on a baking sheet.
9) Fill ramekins with Crème Brûlée mixture, liquid slightly below the rim.
10) Bake using the Direct Heat method, checking every 5 minutes.
11) Once the mixture is slightly solidified, remove the baking sheet from the oven. Allow ramekins to cool down at room temperature for 5 - 10 minutes and refrigerate. When Brûlée is cold, caramelize (i.e. melt) the sugar and serve.

Beet Crème Brûlée

42 g thinly sliced beets, skins removed	210 g thinly sliced beets, skins removed
90 ml whipping cream	450 ml whipping cream
60 ml whipping cream	300 ml whipping cream
24 g sugar	120 g sugar
90 ml milk	450 ml milk
2 1/2 egg yolks (48 g)	12 egg yolks (240 g)
1/3 egg (17 - 19 g)	1 1/2 eggs (84 - 93 g)

Yield: 6 x 2 oz approx. **Yield:** 30 x 2 oz approx.

The recipe below is in small quantities. Please change the amount of cream and milk required for large quantities.

1) In a pot, bring 90 ml cream and 42 g beet to a rolling boil. Cook beets on medium heat until soft, liquid almost evaporated. Remove from heat. Set it aside.
2) In a food processor or blender, purée beets with 90 ml milk until smooth. Set it aside.
3) In a pot, bring cream 60 ml cream to a rolling boil. Remove from heat. Set it aside.
4) In a mixing bowl, combine eggs (both yolks and egg(s)) and sugar. Whisk until thoroughly blended .
5) Slowly pour and whisk the hot cream into the egg mixture. Whisk until thoroughly blended.
6) Whisk the beet purée into the cream mixture. Whisk until thoroughly blended.
7) Put ramekins on a baking sheet.
8) Fill ramekins with Crème Brûlée mixture, liquid slightly below the rim.
9) Bake using the Direct Heat method, checking every 5 minutes.
10) Once the mixture is slightly solidified, remove the baking sheet from the oven. Allow ramekins to cool down at room temperature for 5 - 10 minutes and refrigerate. When Brûlée is cold, caramelize (i.e. melt) the sugar and serve.

Blueberry and Butter Crème Brûlée

188 ml whipping cream	750 ml whipping cream
94 ml milk	375 ml milk
150 g frozen blueberry purée or fresh blueberries	600 g frozen blueberry purée or fresh blueberries
56 g melted butter	225 g melted butter
38 g sugar	150 g sugar
2 1/4 eggs yolks (45 g)	9 egg yolks (180 g)
3/4 egg (42 - 47 g)	3 eggs (168 - 186 g)
Yield: 7 x 2 oz approx.	**Yield:** 28 x 2 oz approx.

1) In a pot, bring cream, milk, butter and blueberry purée to a rolling boil (if using fresh blueberry, purée blueberry with milk until smooth in a food processor or blender). Remove from heat. Set it aside.
2) In a mixing bowl, combine eggs (both yolks and egg(s)) and sugar. Whisk until thoroughly blended.
3) Slowly pour and whisk the hot cream mixture into the egg mixture. Whisk until thoroughly blended.
4) Put ramekins on a baking sheet.
5) Fill ramekins with Crème Brûlée mixture, liquid slightly below the rim.
6) Bake using the Direct Heat method, checking every 5 minutes.
7) Once the mixture is slightly solidified, remove the baking sheet from the oven. Allow ramekins to cool down at room temperature for 5 - 10 minutes and refrigerate. When Brûlée is cold, caramelize (i.e. melt) the sugar and serve.

Caramel Apple Crème Brûlée

130 g caramelized apples	400 g caramelized apples
65 ml milk	200 ml milk
16 g sugar	50 g sugar
130 ml whipping cream	400 ml whipping cream
1/3 egg (18 - 21 g)	1 egg (56 - 62 g)
1 1/3 egg yolks (27 g)	4 egg yolks (80 g)

Yield: 7 x 2 oz approx. **Yield:** 22 x 2 oz approx.

1) In a food processor or blender, purée caramelized apples and milk until smooth. Set it aside.
2) In a pot, bring cream to a rolling boil. Remove from heat. Set it aside.
3) In a mixing bowl, combine eggs (both yolks and egg(s)) and sugar. Whisk until thoroughly blended.
4) Slowly pour and whisk the hot cream into the egg mixture. Whisk until thoroughly blended.
5) Whisk the apple mixture into the cream mixture. Whisk until thoroughly blended.
6) Put ramekins on a baking sheet.
7) Fill ramekins with Crème Brûlée mixture, liquid slightly below the rim.
8) Bake using the Direct Heat method, checking every 5 minutes.
9) Once the mixture is slightly solidified, remove the baking sheet from the oven. Allow ramekins to cool down at room temperature for 5 - 10 minutes and refrigerate. When Brûlée is cold, caramelize (i.e. melt) the sugar and serve.

Caramelized Apple

65 g butter
100 g sugar
550 g peeled apples

In a stainless steel frying pan, caramelize the sugar with a wooden spoon on medium heat until the sugar starts to turn brown and melted (stir constantly otherwise the sugar will burn). Once the sugar is melted, remove from heat. Add the butter to the caramelized sugar and stir until butter is melted. Set it aside. With the peeled apples, cut the apples into quarters and remove the core. Put the quartered apples on top of the caramelized sugar, assembling the apples in circles. Once the apples are in the frying pan, bake the apples for 30 minutes to 1 hour at 300°F (148°C) until golden brown.

Caramel Candy Crème Brûlée

136 ml whipping cream
33 ml milk
1 1/2 egg yolks (33 g)
33 g soft caramel candies

Yield: 6 x 2 oz approx.

500 ml whipping cream
120 ml milk
6 egg yolks (120 g)
120 g soft caramel candies

Yield: 22 x 2 oz approx.

1) Chop the caramel candies into very small pieces (approximately 2 mm x 2 mm) and place in a mixing bowl. Set it aside.
2) In a pot, bring cream and milk to a rolling boil. Remove from heat. Pour the hot cream over the caramel candies. Whisk slowly until the candies are melted and thoroughly blended. Set it aside.
3) In a mixing bowl, combine egg yolks and sugar. Whisk until thoroughly blended.
4) Whisk the cream mixture into the egg mixture. Whisk until thoroughly blended.
5) Put ramekins on a baking sheet.
6) Fill ramekins with Crème Brûlée mixture, liquid slightly below the rim.
7) Bake using the Direct Heat method, checking every 5 minutes.
8) Once the mixture is slightly solidified, remove the baking sheet from the oven. Allow ramekins to cool down at room temperature for 5 - 10 minutes and refrigerate. When Brûlée is cold, caramelize (i.e. melt) the sugar and serve.

Recipe: courtesy of Professor Florent Cantaut of Gastronomicom, Agde, France.

Carrot and Cumin Crème Brûlée

1.3 g cumin seeds	5 g cumin seeds
75 g carrots peeled	300 g carrots peeled
175 ml whipping cream	700 ml whipping cream
100 ml milk	400 ml milk
2 egg yolks (40 g)	8 egg yolks (160 g)
1/2 egg (28 - 31 g)	2 eggs (112 - 124 g)
25 g sugar	100 g sugar

Yield: 6 x 2 oz approx.   **Yield:** 24 x 2 oz approx.

1) Add carrots to a pot, cover with water and bring carrots to a simmering boil on medium heat. Cook until tender (knife can pierce through). Strain and set it aside.
2) In a frying pan on medium heat, sauté the cumin seeds for approximately 2 minutes until you smell the aroma. Remove from heat. Put the seeds in a small bowl and set it aside.
3) In a food processor or blender, purée carrots, cumin seeds and milk until smooth.
4) In a pot, bring cream to a rolling boil. Remove from heat. Set it aside.
5) In a mixing bowl, combine eggs (both yolks and egg(s)) and sugar. Whisk until thoroughly blended.
6) Slowly pour and whisk the hot cream into the egg mixture. Whisk until thoroughly blended.
7) Whisk the carrot mixture into the cream mixture. Whisk until thoroughly blended.
8) Put ramekins on a baking sheet.
9) Fill ramekins with Crème Brûlée mixture, liquid slightly below the rim.
10) Bake using the Direct Heat method, checking every 5 minutes.
11) Once the mixture is slightly solidified, remove the baking sheet from the oven. Allow ramekins to cool down at room temperature for 5 - 10 minutes and refrigerate. When Brûlée is cold, caramelize (i.e. melt) the sugar and serve.

Chocolate and Chili Crème Brûlée

150 ml whipping cream	900 ml whipping cream
50 ml milk	300 ml milk
0.8 g chili pepper powder	4.5 g chili pepper powder
15 g sugar	90 g sugar
1 1/2 egg yolks (30 g)	9 egg yolks (180 g)
1/2 egg (28 - 31 g)	3 eggs (168 - 186 g)
38 g dark chocolate chips (if using chocolate chunks, chop into small pieces)	225 g dark chocolate chips (if using chocolate chunks, chop into small pieces)

Yield: 6 x 2 oz approx.   **Yield:** 33 x 2 oz approx.

1) Put chocolate chips or pieces in a mixing bowl and set it aside.
2) In a pot, bring cream and milk to a rolling boil. Remove from heat. Pour the hot cream over the chocolate. Whisk slowly until the chocolate is melted and thoroughly blended. Set it aside.
3) In a mixing bowl, combine eggs (both yolks and egg(s)), chili powder, and sugar. Whisk until thoroughly blended.
4) Slowly pour and whisk the chocolate mixture into the egg mixture. Whisk until thoroughly blended.
5) Put ramekins on a baking sheet.
6) Fill ramekins with Crème Brûlée mixture, liquid slightly below the rim.
7) Bake using the Direct Heat method, checking every 5 minutes.
8) Once the mixture is slightly solidified, remove the baking sheet from the oven. Allow ramekins to cool down at room temperature for 5 - 10 minutes and refrigerate. When Brûlée is cold, caramelize (i.e. melt) the sugar and serve.

Chocolate Chip Cookie Crème Brûlée

125 ml milk
360 ml whipping cream
50 g chocolate chip cookies
50 g sugar
5 egg yolks (100 g)

500 ml milk
1440 ml whipping cream
200 g chocolate chip cookies
200 g sugar
17 egg yolks (340 g)

Yield: 8 x 2 oz approx.

Yield: 32 x 2 oz approx.

1) In a food processor or blender, purée the chocolate chip cookies with milk until smooth. Set it aside.
2) In a pot, bring cream to a rolling boil. Remove from heat. Set it aside.
3) In a mixing bowl, combine egg yolks and sugar. Whisk until thoroughly blended.
4) Slowly pour and whisk the hot cream into the egg mixture. Whisk until thoroughly blended.
5) Whisk the cookie mixture into the cream mixture.
6) Put ramekins on a baking sheet.
7) Fill ramekins with Crème Brûlée mixture, liquid slightly below the rim.
8) Bake using the Direct Heat method, checking every 5 minutes.
9) Once the mixture is slightly solidified, remove the baking sheet from the oven. Allow ramekins to cool down at room temperature for 5 - 10 minutes and refrigerate. When Brûlée is cold, caramelize (i.e. melt) the sugar and serve.

Chocolate and Mint Crème Brûlée

6 g fresh pepper mint or 3 ml pepper mint extract	16 g fresh pepper mint or 7.5 ml pepper mint extract
300 ml whipping cream	900 ml whipping cream
85 ml milk	250 ml milk
33 g sugar	100 g sugar
4 egg yolks (80 g)	12 egg yolks (240 g)
60 g dark chocolate chips (if using chocolate chunks, chop into small pieces)	180 g dark chocolate chips (if using chocolate chunks, chop into small pieces)
Yield: 7 x 2 oz approx.	**Yield:** 28 x 2 oz approx.

The recipe below is in small quantities. Please change the amount of cream and milk required for large quantities.

1) Put chocolate chips or pieces into a mixing bowl and set it aside.
2) In a pot, bring 300 ml cream and 85 ml milk to a rolling boil. Remove from heat. Infuse the sachet of fresh mint leaves in the hot cream (see page 40 for infusion instructions). Cool the cream in an ice bath (see page 42 for ice bath instructions). Cover with plastic wrap and refrigerate over night (if using mint extract, omit the infusion, add mint extract to the cream and continue with step 5).
3) After the infusion time, remove the sachet of fresh mint and squeeze as much liquid out as possible back into the cream.
4) In a measuring cup, re-measure the cream to 385 ml. Add more cream if necessary to reach 385 ml.
5) In a pot, bring infused cream to a rolling boil. Remove from heat. Pour hot cream over the chocolate. Whisk slowly until chocolate is melted and thoroughly blended.
6) In a mixing bowl, combine eggs (both yolks and egg(s)) and sugar. Whisk until thoroughly blended.
7) Slowly pour and whisk the chocolate cream mixture into the egg mixture. Whisk until thoroughly blended.
8) Put ramekins on a baking sheet.
9) Fill ramekins with Crème Brûlée mixture, liquid slightly below the rim.
10) Bake using the Direct Heat method, checking every 5 minutes.
11) Once the mixture is slightly solidified, remove the baking sheet from the oven. Allow ramekins to cool down at room temperature for 5 - 10 minutes and refrigerate. When Brûlée is cold, caramelize (i.e. melt) the sugar and serve.

Chocolate and Orange Crème Brûlée

115 ml whipping cream	500 ml whipping cream
45 ml milk	200 ml milk
68 g orange juice concentrate	300 g orange juice concentrate
27 g sugar	120 g sugar
40 g dark chocolate chips (if using chocolate chunks, chop into small pieces)	175 g dark chocolate chips (if using chocolate chunks, chop into small pieces)
1 3/4 egg yolks (35 g)	8 egg yolks (160 g)
1/2 egg (28 - 31 g)	2 eggs (112 - 124 g)

Yield: 6 x 2 oz approx. **Yield:** 26 x 2 oz approx.

1) Put chocolate chips or pieces into a mixing bowl and set it aside.
2) In a pot, bring orange juice, milk, and cream to a rolling boil. Remove from heat.
3) Pour the hot cream mixture over the chocolate. Whisk slowly until chocolate is melted and thoroughly blended. Set it aside.
4) In a mixing bowl, combine eggs (both yolks and egg(s)) and sugar. Whisk until thoroughly blended.
5) Slowly pour and whisk the chocolate cream mixture into the egg mixture. Whisk until thoroughly blended.
6) Put ramekins on a baking sheet.
7) Fill ramekins with Crème Brûlée mixture, liquid slightly below the rim.
8) Bake using the Direct Heat method, checking every 5 minutes.
9) Once the mixture is slightly solidified, remove the baking sheet from the oven. Allow ramekins to cool down at room temperature for 5 - 10 minutes and refrigerate. When Brûlée is cold, caramelize (i.e. melt) the sugar and serve.

Chocolate and Raspberry Crème Brûlée

33 g dark chocolate chips (if using chocolate chunks, chop into small pieces)	150 g dark chocolate chips (if using chocolate chunks, chop into small pieces)
42 g raspberry purée	188 g raspberry purée
100 ml whipping cream	450 ml whipping cream
65 ml milk	300 ml milk
20 g sugar	90 g sugar
1 1/4 egg yolks (25 g)	9 egg yolks (180 g)
3/4 egg (42 - 47 g)	3 eggs (168 - 186 g)

Yield: 6 x 2 oz approx.   **Yield:** 27 x 2 oz approx.

1) Put chocolate chips or pieces into a mixing bowl and set it aside.
2) In a pot, bring cream, raspberry purée, and milk to a rolling boil.
3) Pour hot cream mixture over the chocolate. Whisk until chocolate is melted and thoroughly blended.
4) In a mixing bowl, combine eggs (both yolks and egg(s)) and sugar. Whisk until thoroughly blended.
5) Slowly pour and whisk the chocolate cream mixture into the egg mixture. Whisk until thoroughly blended.
6) Put ramekins on a baking sheet.
7) Fill ramekins with Crème Brûlée mixture, liquid slightly below the rim.
8) Bake using the Direct Heat method, checking every 5 minutes.
9) Once the mixture is slightly solidified, remove the baking sheet from the oven. Allow ramekins to cool down at room temperature for 5 - 10 minutes and refrigerate. When Brûlée is cold, caramelize (i.e. melt) the sugar and serve.

Chokecherry Crème Brûlée

65 ml chokecherry juice	350 ml chokecherry juice
115 whipping cream	600 ml whipping cream
75 ml milk	400 ml milk
2 egg yolks (40 g)	10 egg yolks (200 g)
1/3 egg (19 - 21 g)	2 eggs (112 - 124 g)
28 g sugar	150 g sugar

Yield: 6 x 2 oz approx.   **Yield:** 32 x 2 oz approx.

1) In a pot, bring chokecherry juice, cream, and milk to a rolling boil. Set it aside.
2) In a mixing bowl, combine eggs (both yolks and egg(s)) and sugar. Whisk until thoroughly blended.
3) Slowly pour and whisk the chokecherry cream mixture into the egg mixture. Whisk until thoroughly blended.
4) Put ramekins on a baking sheet.
5) Fill ramekins with Crème Brûlée mixture, liquid slightly below the rim.
6) Bake using the Direct Heat method, checking every 5 minutes.
7) Once the mixture is slightly solidified, remove the baking sheet from the oven. Allow ramekins to cool down at room temperature for 5 - 10 minutes and refrigerate. When Brûlée is cold, caramelize (i.e. melt) the sugar and serve.

Chokecherry Juice
Chokecherry cannot be found in your local stores. You might be able to find chokecherries in specialty shops. Chokecherries can be picked in the summer. Please do not pick the berries unless you are a confident forager or find someone who can identify them. Digesting the wrong berries can be fatal. To make chokecherry juice, fill a large pot with chokecherries, cover the berries with water, and bring to a boil on medium to high heat. Once the berries are opened, strain and squeeze the berries to extract as much juice as possible.

Cinnamon and Maple Syrup Crème Brûlée

250 ml whipping cream
100 ml milk
50 ml maple syrup
3 egg yolks (60 g)

1000 ml whipping cream
500 ml milk
250 ml maple syrup
15 egg yolks (300 g)

Yield: 6 x 2 oz approx.

Yield: 30 x 2 oz approx.

1) In a pot, bring cream and milk to a rolling boil. Set it aside.
2) In a mixing bowl, combine egg yolks, cinnamon, and maple syrup. Whisk until thoroughly blended.
3) Slowly pour and whisk the hot cream mixture into the egg mixture. Whisk until thoroughly blended.
4) Put ramekins on a baking sheet.
5) Fill ramekins with Crème Brûlée mixture, liquid slightly below the rim.
6) Bake using the Direct Heat method, checking every 5 minutes.
7) Once the mixture is slightly solidified, remove the baking sheet from the oven. Allow ramekins to cool down at room temperature for 5 - 10 minutes and refrigerate. When Brûlée is cold, caramelize (i.e. melt) the sugar and serve.

Coconut Crème Brûlée

190 ml whipping cream	750 ml whipping cream
265 g coconut milk	1050 g coconut milk
2 1/2 egg yolks (50 g)	15 egg yolks (300 g)
3/4 egg (42 - 47 g)	3 eggs (168 - 184 g)
56 g sugar	225 g sugar

Yield: 6 x 2 oz approx.   **Yield:** 24 x 2 oz approx.

1) In a pot, bring cream and coconut milk to a rolling boil. Remove from heat. Set it aside.
2) In a mixing bowl, combine eggs (both yolks and egg(s)) and sugar. Whisk until thoroughly blended.
3) Slowly pour and whisk the hot cream mixture into the egg mixture. Whisk until thoroughly blended.
4) Put ramekins on a baking sheet.
5) Fill ramekins with Crème Brûlée mixture, liquid slightly below the rim.
6) Bake using the Direct Heat method, checking every 5 minutes.
7) Once the mixture is slightly solidified, remove the baking sheet from the oven. Allow ramekins to cool down at room temperature for 5 - 10 minutes and refrigerate. When Brûlée is cold, caramelize (i.e. melt) the sugar and serve.

Coconut and Vanilla Crème Brûlée

100 ml whipping cream	400 ml whipping cream
165 ml coconut milk	660 ml coconut milk
40 g sugar	160 g sugar
2 egg yolks (40 g)	8 egg yolks (160 g)
2/3 egg (38 - 42 g)	3 eggs (152 - 168 g)
1 vanilla bean	4 vanilla beans

Yield: 6 x 2 oz approx.   **Yield:** 24 x 2 oz approx.

1) Split the vanilla bean(s) in half with a knife. With the back of the knife, scrape out the vanilla pods. Put the vanilla pods and vanilla bean(s) in a pot with cream and coconut milk. Bring to a rolling boil. Remove from heat. Set it aside.
2) In a mixing bowl, combine eggs (both yolks and egg(s)) and sugar. Whisk until thoroughly blended.
3) Remove the vanilla bean(s). Squeeze as much liquid out as possible back into the cream and discard the bean(s). Slowly pour and whisk the hot cream mixture into the egg mixture. Whisk until thoroughly blended.
4) Put ramekins on a baking sheet.
5) Fill ramekins with Crème Brûlée mixture, liquid slightly below the rim.
6) Bake using the Direct Heat method, checking every 5 minutes.
7) Once the mixture is slightly solidified, remove the baking sheet from the oven. Allow ramekins to cool down at room temperature for 5 - 10 minutes and refrigerate. When Brûlée is cold, caramelize (i.e. melt) the sugar and serve.

Cranberry Crème Brûlée

50 ml milk	300 ml milk
125 ml whipping cream	500 ml whipping cream
170 g fresh or frozen cranberries	680 g fresh or frozen cranberries
100 ml milk	400 ml milk
3 egg yolks (60 g)	12 egg yolks (240 g)
1/2 egg (28 - 31 g)	2 eggs (112 - 124 g)
50 g sugar	200 g sugar

Yield: 8 x 2 oz approx.   **Yield:** 32 x 2 oz approx.

The recipe below is in small quantities. Please change the amount of cream and milk required for large quantities. In step 2, add cream to reach 1000 ml for large quantities.**

1) On medium heat, simmer 170 g cranberries with 50 ml milk and 125 ml cream for 30 minutes until cranberries are soft and opened. Remove from heat, purée the cranberries and strain, reserving the liquid.
2) In a measuring cup with 100 ml milk, add cranberry liquid. Add cream to reach 250 ml.
3) In a pot bring the cranberry cream mixture to a rolling boil. Remove from heat. Set it aside.
4) In mixing bowl, combine eggs (both yolks and egg(s)) and sugar. Whisk until thoroughly blended.
5) Slowly pour and whisk the hot cream mixture into the egg mixture. Whisk until thoroughly blended.
6) Put ramekins on a baking sheet.
7) Fill ramekins with Crème Brûlée mixture, liquid slightly below the rim.
8) Bake using the Direct Heat method, checking every 5 minutes.
9) Once the mixture is slightly solidified, remove the baking sheet from the oven. Allow ramekins to cool down at room temperature for 5 - 10 minutes and refrigerate. When Brûlée is cold, caramelize (i.e. melt) the sugar and serve.

Dragon Fruit Crème Brûlée

75 ml whipping cream	300 ml whipping cream
75 ml milk	300 ml milk
175 g dragon fruit meat	700 g dragon fruit meat
45 g sugar	180 g sugar
2 1/2 egg yolks (50 g)	10 egg yolks (200 g)
1/2 egg (28 - 31 g)	2 eggs (112 - 124 g)

Yield: 8 x 2 oz approx.   **Yield:** 32 x 2 oz approx.

1) In a food processor or blender, purée the dragon fruit until smooth. Set it aside.
2) In a pot, bring cream and milk to a rolling boil. Remove from heat and set it aside.
3) In a mixing bowl, combine eggs (both yolks and egg(s)) and sugar. Whisk until thoroughly blended.
4) Slowly pour and whisk the hot cream mixture into the egg mixture. Whisk until thoroughly blended.
5) Whisk the dragon fruit purée into the cream mixture. Whisk until thoroughly blended.
6) Put ramekins on a baking sheet.
7) Fill ramekins with Crème Brûlée mixture, liquid slightly below the rim.
8) Bake using the Direct Heat method, checking every 5 minutes.
9) Once the mixture is slightly solidified, remove the baking sheet from the oven. Allow ramekins to cool down at room temperature for 5 - 10 minutes and refrigerate. When Brûlée is cold, caramelize (i.e. melt) the sugar and serve.

Early Grey Tea Crème Brûlée

55 ml milk	250 ml milk
275 ml whipping cream	1200 ml whipping cream
57 g sugar	250 g sugar
3 1/2 egg yolks (70 g)	15 egg yolks (300 g)
1/2 egg (28 - 31 g)	2 eggs (112 - 124 g)
0.9 g Early Grey loose tea leaves or 1 bag	4 g Early Grey loose tea leaves or 2 bags

Yield: 6 x 2 oz approx.   **Yield:** 26 x 2 oz approx.

The recipe below is in small quantities. Please change the amount of cream and milk required for large quantities.

1) In a pot, bring 275 ml cream and 55 ml milk to a rolling boil. Remove from heat. Infuse the sachet of loose tea leaves or tea bags in the hot liquid for 15 minutes (see page 40 for infusion instructions).
2) After the infusion time, remove the sachet and squeeze as much liquid as possible back to the cream.
3) In a measuring cup, re-measure the infused cream to 330 ml. Add cream if necessary.
4) In a pot, bring the infused cream to a rolling boil. Remove from heat and set it aside.
5) In a mixing bowl, combine eggs (both yolks and egg(s)) and sugar. Whisk until thoroughly blended.
6) Slowly pour and whisk the hot infused cream mixture into the egg mixture. Whisk until thoroughly blended.
7) Put ramekins on a baking sheet.
8) Fill ramekins with Crème Brûlée mixture, liquid slightly below the rim.
9) Bake using the Direct Heat method, checking every 5 minutes.
10) Once the mixture is slightly solidified, remove the baking sheet from the oven. Allow ramekins to cool down at room temperature for 5 - 10 minutes and refrigerate. When Brûlée is cold, caramelize (i.e. melt) the sugar and serve.

Eggnog Crème Brûlée

200 ml eggnog
20 ml rum liqour
2 1/2 egg yolks (50 g)
1 /2 egg (28 - 31 g)
30 g sugar

Yield: 6 x 2 oz approx.

1000 ml eggnog
100 ml rum liqour
12 egg yolks (240 g)
2 eggs (112 - 124 g)
150 g sugar

Yield: 30 x 2 oz approx.

1) In a mixing bowl, combine eggs (both yolks and egg(s)) and sugar. Whisk until thoroughly blended.
2) Whisk the eggnog and rum into the egg mixture. Whisk until thoroughly blended.
3) Put ramekins on a baking sheet.
4) Fill ramekins with Crème Brûlée mixture, liquid slightly below the rim.
5) Bake using the Direct Heat method, checking every 5 minutes.
6) Once the mixture is slightly solidified, remove the baking sheet from the oven. Allow ramekins to cool down at room temperature for 5 - 10 minutes and refrigerate. When Brûlée is cold, caramelize (i.e. melt) the sugar and serve.

Espresso Crème Brûlée

185 ml whipping cream
65 ml milk
20 ml espresso
30 g sugar
2 1/4 egg yolks (45 g)

Yield: 7 x 2 oz approx.

750 ml whipping cream
265 ml milk
75 ml espresso
120 g sugar
9 egg yolks (180 g)

Yield: 28 x 2 oz approx.

1) In a pot, bring cream and milk to a rolling boil. Remove from heat and set it aside.
2) In a mixing bowl, combine egg yolks and sugar. Whisk until thoroughly blended.
3) Slowly pour and whisk the hot cream mixture into the egg mixture. Whisk until thoroughly blended.
4) Whisk the espresso into the cream mixture. Whisk until thoroughly blended.
5) Put ramekins on a baking sheet.
6) Fill ramekins with Crème Brûlée mixture, liquid slightly below the rim.
7) Bake using the Direct Heat method, checking every 5 minutes.
8) Once the mixture is slightly solidified, remove the baking sheet from the oven. Allow ramekins to cool down at room temperature for 5 - 10 minutes and refrigerate. When Brûlée is cold, caramelize (i.e. melt) the sugar and serve.

Fig Crème Brûlée

100 g fresh figs	500 g fresh figs
50 ml milk	250 ml milk
30 g sugar	150 g sugar
200 ml whipping cream	1000 ml whipping cream
3 1/2 egg yolks (70 g)	17 1/2 egg yolks (350 g)

Yield: 6 x 2 oz approx. **Yield:** 30 x 2 oz approx.

1) In a food processor or blender, purée the figs with milk until smooth. Set it aside.
2) In a pot, bring cream to a rolling boil. Remove from heat. Set it aside.
3) In a mixing bowl, combine egg yolks and sugar. Whisk until thoroughly blended.
4) Slowly pour and whisk the hot cream into the egg mixture. Whisk until thoroughly blended.
5) Whisk the fig mixture into the cream mixture until thoroughly blended.
6) Put ramekins on a baking sheet.
7) Fill ramekins with Crème Brûlée mixture, liquid slightly below the rim.
8) Bake using the Direct Heat method, checking every 5 minutes.
9) Once the mixture is slightly solidified, remove the baking sheet from the oven. Allow ramekins to cool down at room temperature for 5 - 10 minutes and refrigerate. When Brûlée is cold, caramelize (i.e. melt) the sugar and serve.

Fireball® Whisky Crème Brûlée

40 ml Fireball® whisky	200 ml Fireball® whisky
100 ml whipping cream	500 ml whipping cream
60 ml milk	300 ml milk
1 egg yolk (20 g)	6 egg yolks (120 g)
1/2 egg (28 - 31 g)	2 eggs (112 - 124 g)
30 g sugar	150 g sugar
20 ml Fireball® whisky	100 ml Fireball® whisky

Yield: 6 x 2 oz approx.   **Yield:** 30 x 2 oz approx.

The recipe below is in small quantities. Please change the amount of cream and milk required for large quantities.

1) In a pot, bring 40 ml whisky, 100 ml cream and 60 ml milk to a rolling boil. Remove from heat and set it aside.
2) In a mixing bowl, combine eggs (both yolks and egg(s)) and sugar. Whisk until thoroughly blended.
3) Slowly pour and whisk the hot cream mixture into the egg mixture. Whisk until thoroughly blended.
4) Whisk the rest of the whisky (20 ml) into the cream mixture. Whisk until thoroughly blended.
5) Put ramekins on a baking sheet.
6) Fill ramekins with Crème Brûlée mixture, liquid slightly below the rim.
7) Bake using the Direct Heat method, checking every 5 minutes.
8) Once the mixture is slightly solidified, remove the baking sheet from the oven. Allow ramekins to cool down at room temperature for 5 - 10 minutes and refrigerate. When Brûlée is cold, caramelize (i.e. melt) the sugar and serve.

Foie Gras & Black Truffle Crème Brûlée

150 ml whipping cream	600 ml whipping cream
100 ml milk	400 ml milk
3 egg yolks (60 g)	12 egg yolks (240 g)
120 g foie gras torchon (see foie gras torchon recipe)	480 g foie gras torchon (see foie gras torchon recipe)
1 ml grated black truffles	4 ml grated black truffles

Yield: 6 x 2 oz approx.   **Yield:** 24 x 2 oz approx.

1) In a pot, bring cream and foie gras torchon to a rolling boil on medium heat. Stir constantly to prevent the foie gras from sticking to the pot as foie gras is melted. Remove from heat and set it aside.
2) In a mixing bowl, combine egg yolks, black truffles, and milk. Whisk until thoroughly blended.
3) Slowly pour and whisk the cream mixture into the egg mixture. Whisk until thoroughly blended.
4) Put ramekins on a baking sheet.
5) Fill ramekins with Crème Brûlée mixture, liquid slightly below the rim.
6) Bake using the Direct Heat method, checking every 5 minutes.
7) Once the mixture is slightly solidified, remove the baking sheet from the oven. Allow ramekins to cool down at room temperature for 5 - 10 minutes and refrigerate. When Brûlée is cold, caramelize (i.e. melt) the sugar and serve.

** Foie gras & black truffle Crème Brûlée is a savoury dish with a touch of sweetness. It is an appetizer: a spread like a pâté, and it`s not meant for a dessert. The Crème Brûlée and Fois Gras Torchon recipes which I have included is an excellent starter served with jelly, grapes, fruits, and baguette.**

Foie Gras Torchon Crème Brûlée

185 g foie gras (deveined)	550 g foie gras (deveined)
4.3 g salt	13 g salt
0.4 g black pepper	1.2 g black pepper
0.8 g sugar	2.4 g sugar
1.2 g Himalayan sea salt	3.6 g Himalayan sea salt
5 ml Grand Mariner®	15 ml Grand Mariner®
16" x 32" cheese clothes	16" x 32" x 2 cheese clothes
2 kg sea salt	4 kg sea salt

Yield: 160 g approx.   **Yield:** 480 g approx.

1) In a bowl, pull the foie gras apart to remove all veins, sinews, and blood clots. Set it aside.
2) In a mortar and pestle, pound the Himalayan sea salt to a fine powder.
3) Add the Himalayan sea salt and the rest of the ingredients to the foie gras.
4) Using your hands, mix all the ingredients together until thoroughly blended. The mixture should be smooth. Let the mixture marinate in the refrigerator for 2 hours. Divide the mixture in half.
5) Lay down the piece of cheesecloth. Place the foie gras mixture at one end of the cheesecloth - spreading it evenly across, leaving 3 inches on each side of the cheesecloth and roll up into a cylinder.
6) Twist the ends of the cylinder in opposite directions until the foie gras is secure tightly. Repeat with the rest of foie gras mixture.
7) In a long pan, pour 1 kg of salt. Place the foie gras on top. Cover the foie gras with the rest of the salt. Put the foie gras in the refrigerator and let it rest for 10 hours.
8) Remove the foie gras from the salt. Slowly unroll the cheesecloth.
9) Cut the foie gras into small cylinder and serve with bread, jelly, and fruits.

Garlic and Thyme Crème Brûlée

225 ml whipping cream	900 ml whipping cream
50 ml milk	200 ml milk
40 g sugar	160 g sugar
25 g roasted garlic	100 g roasted garlic
1/2 egg (28 - 31 g)	2 eggs (112 - 124 g)
2 1/2 egg yolks (50 g)	10 egg yolks (200 g)
5 g fresh thyme	20 g fresh thyme

Yield: 8 x 2 oz approx.   **Yield:** 32 x 2 oz approx.

The recipe below is in small quantities. Please change the amount of cream and milk required for large quantities.

1) In a pot, bring 225 ml cream and 50 ml milk to a rolling boil. Remove from heat. Set it aside. Infuse the sachet of thyme in the hot cream for 1 hour (see page 40 for infusion instructions).
2) After the infusion time, remove the sachet and squeeze as much liquid out as possible back into the cream.
3) In a measuring cup, re-measure the cream to 275 ml. Add cream if necessary.
4) In a food processor or blender, purée the infused cream and roasted garlic until smooth.
5) In a pot, bring the infused cream mixture to a rolling boil. Remove from heat. Set it aside.
6) In a mixing bowl, combine eggs (both yolks and egg(s)) and sugar. Whisk until thoroughly blended.
7) Slowly pour and whisk the hot cream mixture into the egg mixture. Whisk until thoroughly blended.
8) Put ramekins on a baking sheet.
9) Fill ramekins with Crème Brûlée mixture, liquid slightly below the rim.
10) Bake using the Direct Heat method, checking every 5 minutes.
11) Once the mixture is slightly solidified, remove the baking sheet from the oven. Allow ramekins to cool down at room temperature for 5 - 10 minutes and refrigerate. When Brûlée is cold, caramelize (i.e. melt) the sugar and serve.

Gooseberry Crème Brûlée

80 ml milk	400 ml milk
120 ml whipping cream	600 ml whipping cream
90 g gooseberry purée	450 g gooseberry purée
20 g sugar	100 g sugar
1 1/2 egg yolks (30 g)	8 egg yolks (160 g)
1/2 egg (28 - 31 g)	2 eggs (112 g - 124 g)

Yield: 7 x 2 oz approx.   **Yield:** 36 x 2 oz approx.

1) In a pot, bring cream and milk to a rolling boil. Remove from heat. Set it aside.
2) In a mixing bowl, combine eggs (both yolks and egg(s)) and sugar. Whisk until thoroughly blended.
3) Slowly pour and whisk the hot cream into the egg mixture. Whisk until thoroughly blended.
4) Whisk the gooseberry purée into the cream mixture. Whisk until thoroughly blended.
5) Put ramekins on a baking sheet.
6) Fill ramekins with Crème Brûlée mixture, liquid slightly below the rim.
7) Bake using the Direct Heat method, checking every 5 minutes.
8) Once the mixture is slightly solidified, remove the baking sheet from the oven. Allow ramekins to cool down at room temperature for 5 - 10 minutes and refrigerate. When Brûlée is cold, caramelize (i.e. melt) the sugar and serve.

Green Apple and Brandy Crème Brûlée

100 g frozen Granny Smith purée or 100 g peeled Granny Smith apples	300 g frozen Granny Smith purée or 300 g peeled Granny Smith apples
125 ml whipping cream	375 ml whipping cream
50 ml milk	150 ml milk
3 egg yolks (60 g)	9 egg yolks (180 g)
1/2 egg (28 - 31 g)	1 1/2 eggs (84 - 93 g)
40 g sugar	120 g sugar
65 ml brandy liqueur	195 ml brandy liqueur

Yield: 8 x 2 oz approx. **Yield:** 24 x 2 oz approx.

1) In a pot, bring cream and Granny Smith apple purée to a rolling boil (if using fresh apples, purée the fruits in a food processor or blender until liquid starts to form). Remove from heat. Set it aside.
2) In a mixing bowl, combine eggs (both yolks and egg(s)) and sugar. Whisk until thoroughly blended.
3) Slowly pour and whisk the hot cream mixture into the egg mixture. Whisk until thoroughly blended.
4) Whisk the apple mixture into the cream mixture. Whisk until thoroughly blended.
5) Put ramekins on a baking sheet.
6) Fill ramekins with Crème Brûlée mixture, liquid slightly below the rim.
7) Bake using the Direct Heat method, checking every 5 minutes.
8) Once the mixture is slightly solidified, remove the baking sheet from the oven. Allow ramekins to cool down at room temperature for 5 - 10 minutes and refrigerate. When Brûlée is cold, caramelize (i.e. melt) the sugar and serve.

Honey and Dill Crème Brûlée

90 g liquid honey	360 g liquid honey
0.5 g dried dill	2 g dried dill
150 ml whipping cream	600 ml whipping cream
100 ml milk	400 ml milk
2 1/2 egg yolks (50 g)	10 egg yolks (200 g)
1/2 egg (28 - 31 g)	2 eggs (112 - 124 g)

Yield: 7 x 2 oz approx.   **Yield:** 28 x 2 oz approx.

1) In a pot, bring cream and milk to a rolling boil. Remove from heat. Set it aside.
2) In a large mixing bowl, combine eggs (both yolks and egg(s)), honey and dill. Whisk until thoroughly blended.
3) Slowly pour and whisk the hot cream into the egg mixture. Whisk until thoroughly blended.
4) Put ramekins on a baking sheet.
5) Fill ramekins with Crème Brûlée mixture, liquid slightly below the rim.
6) Bake using the Direct Heat method, checking every 5 minutes.
7) Once the mixture is slightly solidified, remove the baking sheet from the oven. Allow ramekins to cool down at room temperature for 5 - 10 minutes and refrigerate. When Brûlée is cold, caramelize (i.e. melt) the sugar and serve.

Kahlua® Crème Brûlée

130 ml whipping cream	500 ml whipping cream
5 ml milk	200 ml milk
2 1/2 egg yolks (50 g)	9 egg yolks (180 g)
1/2 egg (28 - 31 g)	2 eggs (112 - 124 g)
32 g sugar	125 g sugar
60 ml Kahlua® liqueur	225 ml Kahlua® liqueur

Yield: 6 x 2 oz approx.　　　　　　　**Yield:** 23 x 2 oz approx.

1) In a pot, bring cream and milk to a rolling boil. Remove from heat. Set it aside.
2) In a mixing bowl, combine eggs (both yolks and egg(s)) and sugar. Whisk until thoroughly blended.
3) Slowly pour and whisk the hot cream into the egg mixture. Whisk until thoroughly blended.
4) Whisk the Kahlua liqueur into the cream mixture. Whisk until thoroughly blended.
5) Put ramekins on a baking sheet.
6) Fill ramekins with Crème Brûlée mixture, liquid slightly below the rim.
7) Bake using the Direct Heat method, checking every 5 minutes.
8) Once the mixture is slightly solidified, remove the baking sheet from the oven. Allow ramekins to cool down at room temperature for 5 - 10 minutes and refrigerate. When Brûlée is cold, caramelize (i.e. melt) the sugar and serve.

Lavender Crème Brûlée

125 ml whipping cream	500 ml whipping cream
100 ml milk	400 ml milk
1 g dried lavender flowers	4 g dried lavender flowers
31 g sugar	125 g sugar
1 1/2 egg yolks (30 g)	6 egg yolks (120 g)
1/2 egg (28 - 31 g)	1 1/2 eggs (84 - 93 g)

Yield: 6 x 2 oz approx.   **Yield:** 23 x 2 oz approx.

The recipe below is in small quantities. Please change the amount of cream and milk required for large quantities.

1) In a pot, bring 125 ml cream and 100 ml milk to a rolling boil. Remove from heat. Infuse sachet of lavender in the hot cream for 15 minutes (see page 40 for infusion instructions). Set it aside.
2) After the infusion time, remove the sachet and squeeze as much liquid out as possible back into the cream.
3) In a measuring cup, re-measure the liquid to 225 ml. Add cream if necessary to reach 225 ml.
4) In a pot, bring the infused cream to a rolling bowl. Remove from heat. Set it aside.
5) In a mixing bowl, combine eggs (both yolks and egg(s)) and sugar. Whisk until thoroughly blended.
6) Slowly pour and whisk the hot infused cream into the egg mixture. Whisk until thoroughly blended.
7) Put ramekins on a baking sheet.
8) Fill ramekins with Crème Brûlée mixture, liquid slightly below the rim.
9) Bake using the Direct Heat method, checking every 5 minutes.
10) Once the mixture is slightly solidified, remove the baking sheet from the oven. Allow ramekins to cool down at room temperature for 5 - 10 minutes and refrigerate. When Brûlée is cold, caramelize (i.e. melt) the sugar and serve.

Lemon and Chardonnay Wine Crème Brûlée

225 ml whipping cream	900 ml whipping cream
25 g lemon zest	100 g lemon zest
100 ml chardonnay wine	400 ml chardonnay wine
3 1/2 egg yolks (70 g)	14 egg yolks (280 g)
1/2 egg (28 - 31 g)	2 eggs (112 -124 g)
35 g sugar	140 g sugar

Yield: 6 x 2 oz approx.   **Yield:** 24 x 2 oz approx.

The recipe below is in small quantities. Please change the amount of cream and milk required for large quantities.

1) In a pot, bring 225 ml cream to a rolling boil. Remove from heat. Infuse the sachet of lemon zest in the hot cream. Set aside and let it infuse for 2 hours (see page 40 for infusion instructions). Cool the cream in an ice bath (see page 42 for ice bath instructions). Cover plastic wrap and refrigerate. After the infusion time, remove the sachet and squeeze as much liquid out as possible back into the cream.
2) In a measuring cup, re-measure it to 225 ml. Add more cream if necessary to reach 225 ml.
3) In a pot, bring the infused cream to a rolling boil. Remove from heat and set it aside.
4) In a mixing bowl, combine eggs (both yolks and egg(s)) and sugar. Whisk until thoroughly blended.
5) Slowly pour and whisk the hot infused cream into the egg mixture. Whisk until thoroughly blended.
6) Whisk the chardonnay wine into the cream mixture.
7) Put ramekins on a baking sheet.
8) Fill ramekins with Crème Brûlée mixture, liquid slightly below the rim.
9) Bake using the Direct Heat method, checking every 5 minutes.
10) Once the mixture is slightly solidified, remove the baking sheet from the oven. Allow ramekins to cool down at room temperature for 5 - 10 minutes and refrigerate. When Brûlée is cold, caramelize (i.e. melt) the sugar and serve.

Lemon, Vanilla, and Cinnamon Crème Brûlée

160 ml whipping cream	475 ml whipping cream
65 ml milk	200 ml milk
65 ml fresh squeezed lemon juice	200 ml fresh squeeze lemon juice
25 g sugar	80 g sugar
2 1/2 egg yolks (50 g)	7 egg yolks (140 g)
2/3 egg (37 - 41 g)	2 eggs (112 - 124 g)
1.6 g cinnamon stick (1 stick)	4.7 g cinnamon stick (2 sticks)
0.7 g lemon zest	2 g lemon zest
0.1 g cinnamon powder	0.3 g cinnamon powder
1 vanilla bean	2 vanilla beans

Yield: 7 x 2 oz approx.   **Yield:** 22 x 2 oz approx.

The recipe below is in small quantities. Please change the amount of cream and milk required for large quantities.

1) Split the vanilla bean(s) in half with a knife. With the back of a knife, scrape out the vanilla pods and put the vanilla pods and bean(s) in a pot with 160 ml cream and 65 ml milk. Bring to a rolling boil. Remove from heat. Infuse the sachet of lemon zest and cinnamon stick(s) in the hot cream. Set aside and let it infuse for 2 hours (see page 40 for infusion instructions). Cool the cream in an ice bath (see page 42 for ice bath instructions). Cover with plastic wrap and refrigerate.
2) After the infusion time, remove the sachet and vanilla bean(s). Squeeze as much liquid out as possible back into the cream and discard the bean(s)
3) In a measuring cup, re-measure the infused cream to 225 ml. Add cream if necessary to reach 225 ml. In a pot, bring the infused cream to a rolling boil and set it aside.
4) In a mixing bowl, combine eggs (both yolks and egg(s)) and sugar. Whisk until thoroughly blended.
5) Slowly pour and whisk the hot infused cream into the egg mixture. Whisk until thoroughly blended.
6) Whisk in the cinnamon powder and lemon juice to the cream mixture. Whisk until thoroughly blended.
7) Put ramekins on a baking sheet.
8) Fill ramekins with Crème Brûlée mixture, liquid slightly below the rim.
9) Bake using the Direct Heat method, checking every 5 minutes.
10) Once the mixture is slightly solidified, remove the baking sheet from the oven. Allow ramekins to cool down at room temperature for 5 - 10 minutes and refrigerate. When Brûlée is cold, caramelize (i.e. melt) the sugar and serve.

Pumpkin Crème Brûlée
Photography by Nik Travisone

Fireball® Whisky Crème Brûlée
Photography by Nik Travisone

Top photo: Lemon and Basil Crème Brûlée, photography by Cam Tran
Bottom photo: Espresso Crème Brûlée, photography by Nik Travisone

Left photo: Lavender Crème Brûlée
Right photo: White Chocolate and Ginger Crème Brûlée
Photography by Nik Travisone

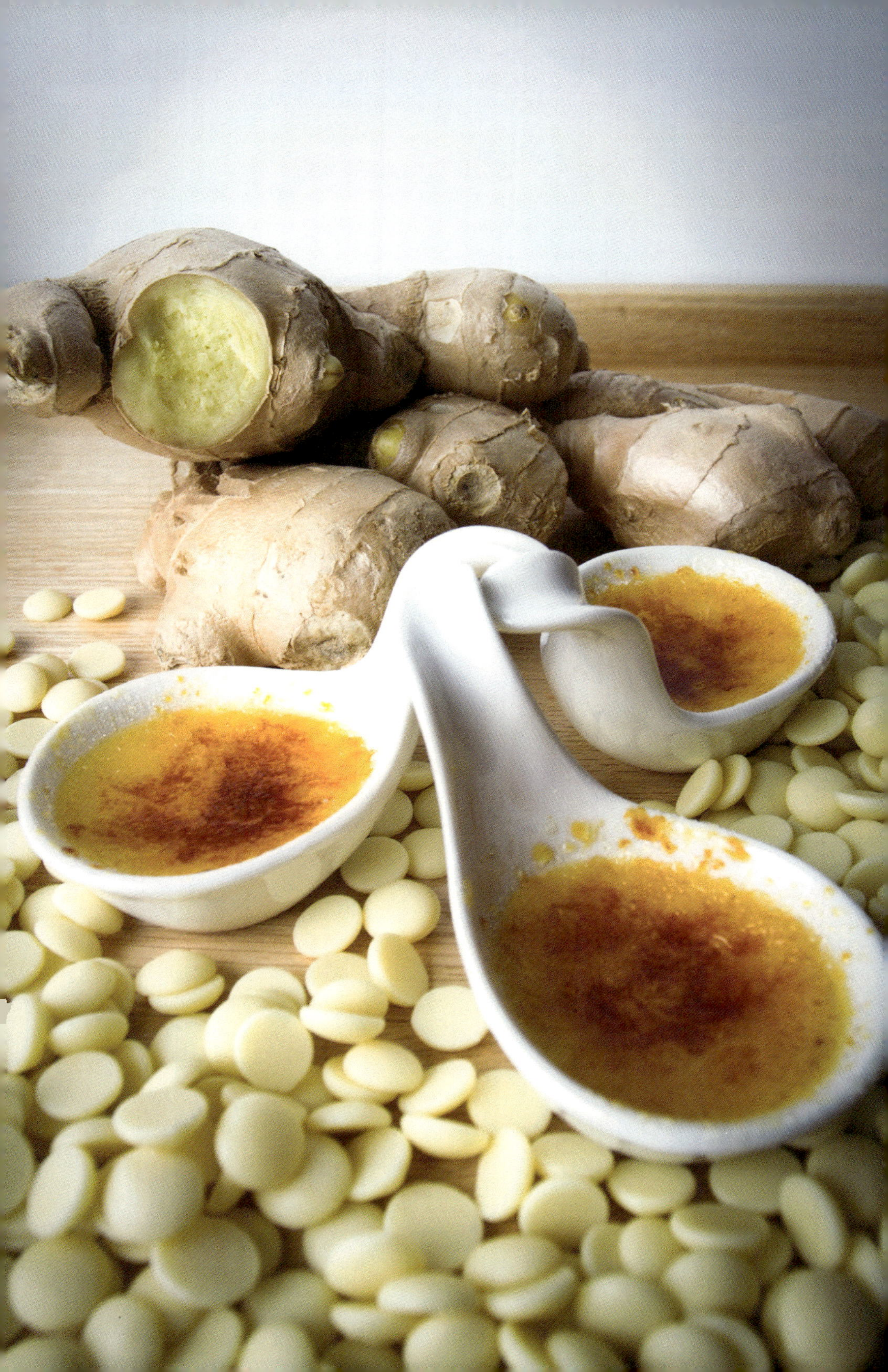

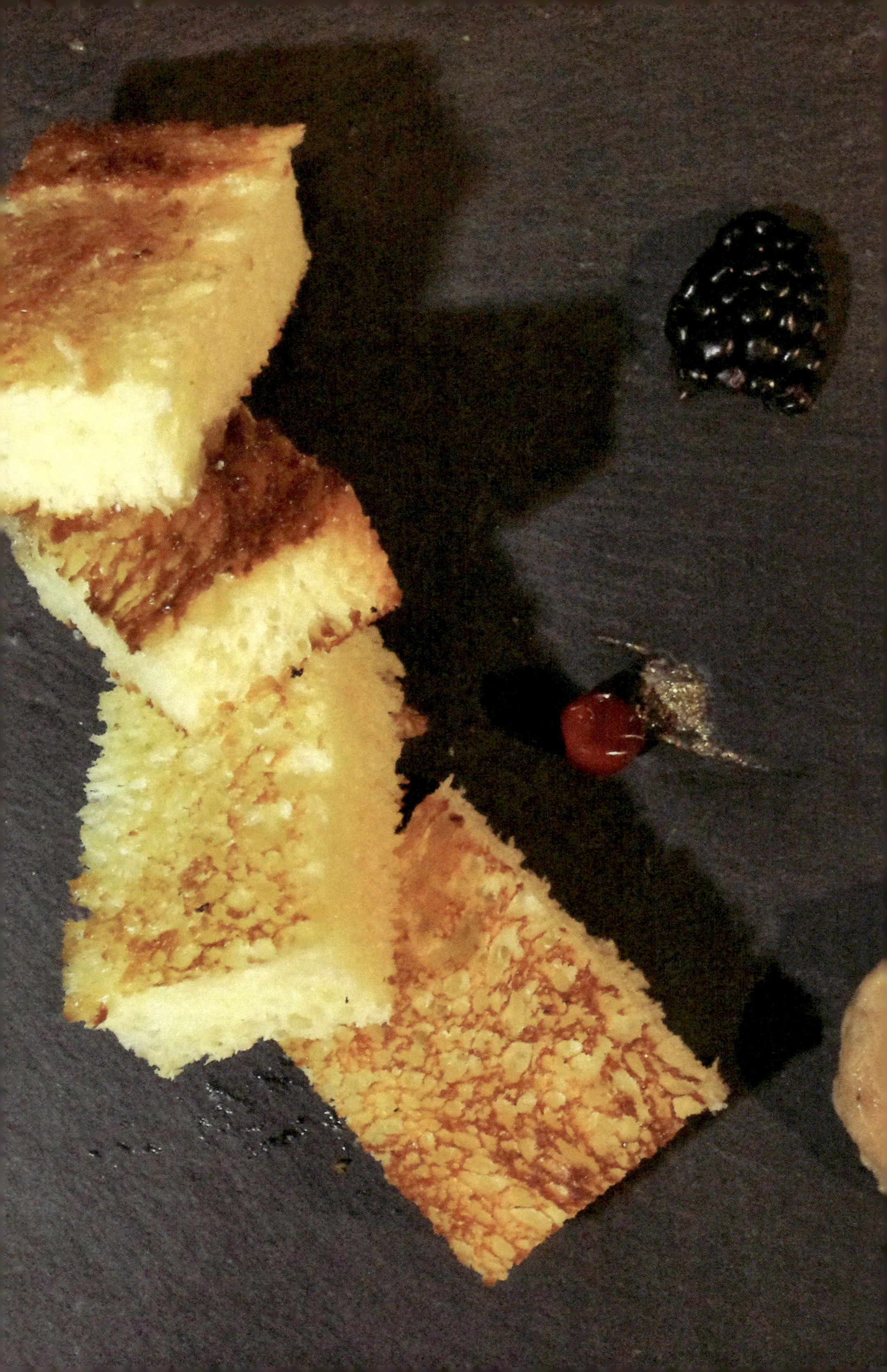

Foie Gras & Black Truffle Crème Brûlée
Photography by Cam Tran

Left photo: Strawberry & Soya Bean Crème Brûlée
Right photo: Lemon & Chardonnay Wine Crème Brûlée
Photography by Nik Travisone

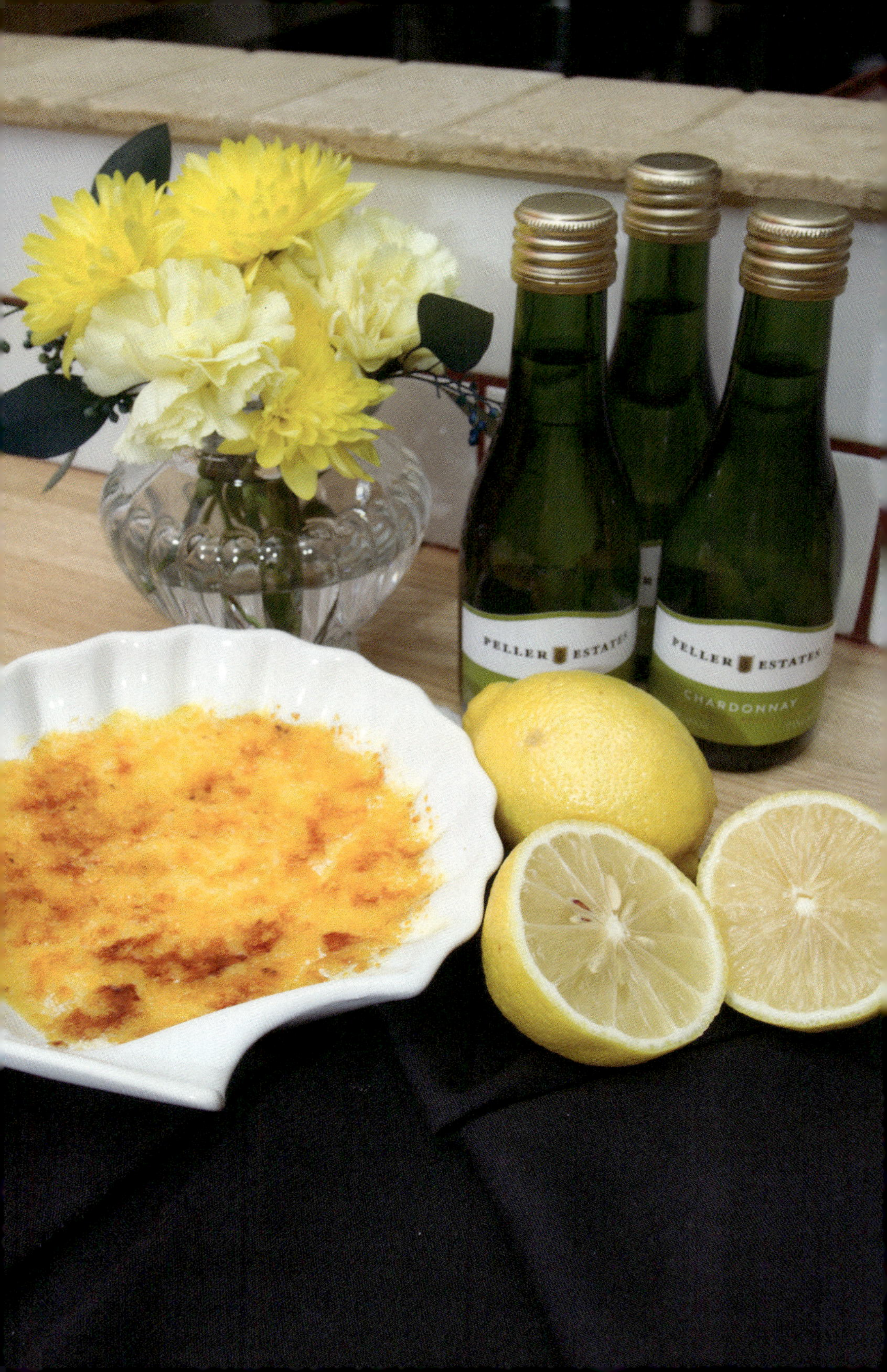
PELLER ESTATES
PELLER ESTATES
CHARDONNAY

Maple Wine Crème Brûlée

115 ml whipping cream	450 ml whipping cream
75 ml milk	300 ml milk
60 ml maple wine	225 ml maple wine
20 ml maple syrup	75 ml maple syrup
3 egg yolks (60 g)	12 egg yolks (240 g)
3/4 egg (42 - 46 g)	3 eggs (168 - 186 g)

Yield: 7 x 2 oz approx.   **Yield:** 26 x 2 oz approx.

1) In a pot, bring cream and milk to a rolling boil. Remove from heat. Set it aside.
2) In a mixing bowl, combine eggs (both yolks and egg(s)) and maple syrup. Whisk until thoroughly blended.
3) Slowly pour and whisk the hot cream into the egg mixture. Whisk until thoroughly blended.
4) Whisk in the maple wine. Whisk until thoroughly blended.
5) Put ramekins on a baking sheet.
6) Fill ramekins with Crème Brûlée mixture, liquid slightly below the rim.
7) Bake using the Direct Heat method, checking every 5 minutes.
8) Once the mixture is slightly solidified, remove the baking sheet from the oven. Allow ramekins to cool down at room temperature for 5 - 10 minutes and refrigerate. When Brûlée is cold, caramelize (i.e. melt) the sugar and serve.

Mochaccino Crème Brûlée

150 ml whipping cream	600 ml whipping cream
75 ml milk	300 ml milk
50 g dark chocolate chips (if using dark chocolate chunks, chop into small pieces)	200 g dark chocolate chips (if using dark chocolate chunks, chop into small pieces)
2 1/2 egg yolks (50 g)	10 egg yolks (200 g)
1/2 egg (28 - 31 g)	2 eggs (112 - 124 g)
35 g sugar	140 g sugar
75 ml espresso	300 ml espresso

Yield: 7 x 2 oz approx.　　　　　　　**Yield:** 28 x 2 oz approx.

1) Put chocolate pieces or chips in a mixing bowl. Set it aside.
2) In a pot, bring cream and milk to a rolling boil. Pour the hot cream over the chocolate. Whisk until chocolate is melted and thoroughly blended. Set it aside.
3) In a mixing bowl, combine eggs (both yolks and egg(s)) and sugar. Whisk until thoroughly blended.
4) Slowly pour and whisk the chocolate cream mixture into the egg mixture. Whisk until thoroughly blended.
5) Whisk the espresso into the cream mixture. Whisk until thoroughly blended.
6) Put ramekins on a baking sheet.
7) Fill ramekins with Crème Brûlée mixture, liquid slightly below the rim.
8) Bake using the Direct Heat method, checking every 5 minutes.
9) Once the mixture is slightly solidified, remove the baking sheet from the oven. Allow ramekins to cool down at room temperature for 5 - 10 minutes and refrigerate. When Brûlée is cold, caramelize (i.e. melt) the sugar and serve.

Orange and Ginger Crème Brûlée

125 ml whipping cream	500 ml whipping cream
19 g fresh grated ginger	75 g fresh grated ginger
30 g sugar	120 g sugar
0.75 g ginger powder	3 g ginger powder
50 ml orange juice concentrate thawed	200 ml orange juice concentrate thawed
1 1/2 egg yolks (30 g)	6 egg yolks (120 g)
1/2 egg (28 - 31 g)	2 eggs (112 - 124 g)

Yield: 5 x 2 oz approx.   **Yield:** 20 x 2 oz approx.

The recipe below is in small quantities. Please change the amount of cream and milk required for large quantities.

1) In a pot, bring 125 ml cream to a rolling boil. Remove from heat. Infuse the sachet of grated ginger in the hot cream. Set it aside and let it infuse for 1 hour (see page 40 for infusion instructions).
2) After the infusion time, remove the sachet and squeeze as much liquid out as possible back into the cream.
3) In a measuring cup, re-measure the cream to 125 ml. Add cream if necessary to reach 125 ml.
4) In a pot, bring the infused cream and orange juice concentrate to a rolling boil. Remove from heat. Set it aside.
5) In a mixing bowl, combine eggs (both yolks and egg(s)), sugar and ginger power. Whisk until thoroughly blended.
6) Slowly pour and whisk the cream mixture into egg mixture. Whisk until thoroughly blended.
7) Put ramekins on a baking sheet.
8) Fill ramekins with Crème Brûlée mixture, liquid slightly below the rim.
9) Bake using the Direct Heat method, checking every 5 minutes.
10) Once the mixture is slightly solidified, remove the baking sheet from the oven. Allow ramekins to cool down at room temperature for 5 - 10 minutes and refrigerate. When Brûlée is cold, caramelize (i.e. melt) the sugar and serve.

Praline Crème Brûlée

85 g praline paste	250 g praline paste
165 ml whipping cream	500 ml whipping cream
65 ml milk	200 ml milk
27 g sugar	80 g sugar
2 1/2 egg yolks (50 g)	7 egg yolks (140 g)
1/3 egg (19 - 21 g)	1 egg (56 - 62 g)
Yield: 7 x 2 oz approx.	**Yield:** 22 x 2 oz approx.

1) In a pot, bring cream, milk and praline paste to a rolling boil. **Stir or whisk constantly to prevent the praline from sticking and burning at the bottom of the pot** Remove from heat. Set it aside.
2) In a mixing bowl, combine eggs (both yolks and egg(s)) and sugar. Whisk until thoroughly blended.
3) Slowly pour and whisk the hot cream mixture into the egg mixture. Whisk until thoroughly blended.
4) Put ramekins on a baking sheet.
5) Fill ramekins with Crème Brûlée mixture, liquid slightly below the rim.
6) Bake using the Direct Heat method, checking every 5 minutes.
7) Once the mixture is slightly solidified, remove the baking sheet from the oven. Allow ramekins to cool down at room temperature for 5 - 10 minutes and refrigerate. When Brûlée is cold, caramelize (i.e. melt) the sugar and serve.

Pumpkin Crème Brûlée

125 ml whipping cream	500 ml whipping cream
50 ml milk	200 ml milk
125 g pumpkin purée	500 g pumpkin purée
3.7 g allspice mixture (see below)	14.6 g allspice mixture (see below)
38 g sugar	150 g sugar
2 egg yolks (40 g)	8 egg yolks (160 g)
1/2 egg (28 - 31 g)	2 eggs (112 - 124 g)

Yield: 7 x 2 oz approx.   **Yield:** 28 x 2 oz approx.

Allspice mixture

1.4 g ginger powder	5.6 g ginger powder
1.3 g cinnamon powder	5 g cinnamon powder
0.75 g nutmeg	3 g nutmeg
0.25 g allspice powder	1 g allspice powder

1) In a pot, bring cream and milk to a rolling boil. Remove from heat. Set it aside.
2) In a mixing bowl, combine eggs (both yolks and egg(s)), sugar, and allspice mixture. Whisk until thoroughly blended.
3) Slowly pour and whisk the hot cream into the egg mixture. Whisk until thoroughly blended.
4) Whisk the pumpkin purée into the cream mixture.
5) Put ramekins on a baking sheet.
6) Fill ramekins with Crème Brûlée mixture, liquid slightly below the rim.
7) Bake using the Direct Heat method, checking every 5 minutes.
8) Once the mixture is slightly solidified, remove the baking sheet from the oven. Allow ramekins to cool down at room temperature for 5 - 10 minutes and refrigerate. When Brûlée is cold, caramelize (i.e. melt) the sugar and serve.

Reeses® Peanut Butter Cup Crème Brûlée

105 g Reeses® Peanut Butter cup chocolate	420 g Reeses® Peanut Butter cup chocolate
150 ml whipping cream	600 ml whipping cream
100 ml milk	400 ml milk
2 egg yolks (40 g)	8 egg yolks (160 g)
1/2 egg (28 - 31 g)	2 eggs (112 - 124 g)
20 g sugar	80 g sugar

Yield: 7 x 2 oz approx.   **Yield:** 28 x 2 oz approx.

1) Chop peanut butter chocolate cups into small pieces and set it aside in a mixing bowl.
2) In a pot, bring cream and milk to a rolling boil. Pour the hot cream over the chocolate. Whisk until chocolate is melted and thoroughly blended. Set it aside.
3) In a mixing bowl, combine eggs (both yolks and egg(s)) and sugar. Whisk until thoroughly blended.
4) Slowly pour and whisk the chocolate cream mixture into the egg mixture. Whisk until thoroughly blended.
5) Put ramekins on a baking sheet.
6) Fill ramekins with Crème Brûlée mixture, liquid slightly below the rim.
7) Bake using the Direct Heat method, checking every 5 minutes.
8) Once the mixture is slightly solidified, remove the baking sheet from the oven. Allow ramekins to cool down at room temperature for 5 - 10 minutes and refrigerate. When Brûlée is cold, caramelize (i.e. melt) the sugar and serve.

Rolo® Crème Brûlée

60 g Rolo® chocolate bar	300 g Rolo® chocolate bar
30 g sugar	150 g sugar
1 1/2 egg yolks (30 g)	8 egg yolks (160 g)
1/2 egg (28 - 31 g)	2 eggs (112 - 124 g)
120 ml whipping cream	600 ml whipping cream
80 ml milk	400 ml milk

Yield: 6 x 2 oz approx.   **Yield:** 30 x 2 oz approx.

1) Chop Rolo® chocolate bar into small pieces. Set it aside in a mixing bowl.
2) In a pot, bring cream and milk to a rolling boil. Pour the hot cream over the chocolate. Whisk until chocolate is melted and thoroughly blended. Set it aside.
3) In a mixing bowl, combine eggs (both yolks and egg(s)) and sugar. Whisk until thoroughly blended.
4) Slowly pour and whisk the chocolate cream mixture into the egg mixture. Whisk until thoroughly blended.
5) Put ramekins on a baking sheet.
6) Fill ramekins with Crème Brûlée mixture, liquid slightly below the rim.
7) Put ramekins on a baking sheet.
8) Bake using the Direct Heat method, checking every 5 minutes.
9) Once the mixture is slightly solidified, remove the baking sheet from the oven. allow ramekins to cool down at room temperature for 5 - 10 minutes and refrigerate. When Brûlée is cold, caramelize (i.e. melt) the sugar and serve.

Rosemary Crème Brûlée

250 ml whipping cream	750 ml whipping cream
125 ml milk	375 ml milk
63 g sugar	190 g sugar
2 1/2 egg yolks (50 g)	7 1/2 egg yolks (150 g)
1/2 egg (28 - 31 g)	1 1/2 eggs (84 - 93 g)
2 g dried rosemary leaves	6 g dried rosemary leaves

Yield: 8 x 2 oz approx.   **Yield:** 24 x 2 oz approx.

The recipe below is in small quantities. Please change the amount of cream and milk required for large quantities.

1) In a pot, bring 250 ml cream and 125 ml milk to a rolling boil. Infuse the sachet of rosemary in the hot cream for 1 hour. Set it aside (see page 40 for infusion instructions).
2) After the infusion time, remove the sachet and squeeze as much liquid out as possible back into the cream.
3) In a measuring cup, re-measure the cream to 375 ml. Add cream if necessary to reach 375 ml.
4) In a pot, bring the infused cream to a rolling boil. Remove from heat. Set it aside.
5) In a mixing bowl, combine eggs (both yolks and egg(s)) and sugar. Whisk until thoroughly blended.
6) Slowly pour and whisk the infused cream into the egg mixture. Whisk until thoroughly blended.
7) Put ramekins on a baking sheet.
8) Fill ramekins with Crème Brûlée mixture, liquid slightly below the rim.
9) Bake using the Direct Heat method, checking every 5 minutes.
10) Once the mixture is slightly solidified, remove the baking sheet from the oven. Allow ramekins to cool down at room temperature for 5 - 10 minutes and refrigerate. When Brûlée is cold, caramelize (i.e. melt) the sugar and serve.

Saffron and Honey Crème Brûlée

44 g liquid honey	220 g liquid honey
2 1/2 egg yolks (50 g)	12 egg yolks (240 g)
1/2 egg (28 - 31 g)	2 eggs (112 - 124 g)
160 ml whipping cream	800 ml whipping cream
80 ml milk	400 ml milk
2 ml or 8 saffron threads	10 ml or 40 saffron threads

Yield: 6 x 2 oz approx.   **Yield:** 30 x 2 oz approx.

The recipe below is in small quantities. Please change the amount of cream and milk required for large quantities.

1) In a pot, bring 160 ml cream and 80 ml milk to a rolling boil. Remove from heat. Infuse the sachet of saffron threads in the hot cream for 25 minutes (see page 40 for infusion instructions). Set it aside.
2) After the infusion time, remove the sachet and squeeze as much liquid out as possible back into the cream.
3) In a measuring cup, re-measure the cream to 240 ml. Add cream if necessary to reach 240 ml.
4) In a pot, bring the infused cream to a rolling boil. Set it aside.
5) In a mixing bowl, combine eggs (both yolks and egg(s)) and honey. Whisk until thoroughly blended.
6) Whisk the infused cream into the egg mixture. Whisk until thoroughly blended.
7) Put ramekins on a baking sheet.
8) Fill ramekins with Crème Brûlée mixture, liquid slightly below the rim.
9) Bake using the Direct Heat method, checking every 5 minutes.
10) Once the mixture is slightly solidified, remove the baking sheet from the oven. Allow ramekins to cool down at room temperature for 5 - 10 minutes and refrigerate. When Brûlée is cold, caramelize (i.e. melt) the sugar and serve.

Strawberry and Soya Bean Crème Brûlée

113 g fresh strawberries	340 g fresh strawberries
43 g cooked soya beans	130 g cooked soya beans
135 ml whipping cream	400 ml whipping cream
35 ml milk	100 ml milk
33 g sugar	100 g sugar
1/3 egg (19 - 21 g)	1 egg (56 - 62 g)
1 3/4 egg yolks (35 g)	5 egg yolks (100 g)

Yield: 7 x 2 oz approx.   **Yield:** 22 x 2 oz approx.

1) In a food processor or blender, purée fresh strawberries, soya beans and milk until smooth. Set it aside.
2) In a pot, bring cream to a rolling boil. Remove from heat. Set it aside.
3) In a mixing bowl, combine eggs (both yolks and egg(s)) and sugar. Whisk until thoroughly blended.
4) Slowly pour and whisk the hot cream into the egg mixture. Whisk until thoroughly blended.
5) Whisk the strawberry and soya bean purée into the cream mixture until thoroughly blended.
6) Put ramekins on a baking sheet.
7) Fill ramekins with Crème Brûlée mixture, liquid slightly below the rim.
8) Bake using the Direct Heat method, checking every 5 minutes.
9) Once the mixture is slightly solidified, remove the baking sheet from the oven. Allow ramekins to cool down at room temperature for 5 - 10 minutes and refrigerate. When Brûlée is cold, caramelize (i.e. melt) the sugar and serve.

Strawberry and Vanilla Crème Brûlée

85 g frozen strawberry purée or fresh strawberries	340 g frozen strawberry purée or fresh strawberries
125 ml whipping cream	500 ml whipping cream
65 ml milk	250 ml milk
25 g sugar	100 g sugar
1/2 egg (28 - 31 g)	2 eggs (112 - 124 g)
2 1/2 egg yolks (50 g)	10 egg yolks (200 g)
1/2 vanilla bean	2 vanilla beans

Yield: 6 x 2 oz approx.   **Yield:** 26 x 2 oz approx.

1) Split the vanilla bean(s) in half with a knife. With the back of a knife, scrape out the vanilla pods. Put the vanilla pods and vanilla bean(s) in a pot with cream, milk and strawberry purée (if using fresh strawberries, purée strawberries and milk until smooth in a food processor or blender). Bring cream mixture to a rolling boil. Remove from heat and set it aside.
2) In a mixing bowl, combine eggs (both yolks and egg(s)) and sugar. Whisk until thoroughly blended.
3) Remove the vanilla bean(s) and squeeze as much liquid out as possible back into the cream and discard the bean(s). Slowly pour and whisk the hot cream mixture into the egg mixture. Whisk until thoroughly blended.
4) Put ramekins on a baking sheet.
5) Fill ramekins with Crème Brûlée mixture, liquid slightly below the rim.
6) Bake using the Direct Heat method, checking every 5 minutes.
7) Once the mixture is slightly solidified, remove the baking sheet from the oven. Allow ramekins to cool down at room temperature for 5 - 10 minutes and refrigerate. When Brûlée is cold, caramelize (i.e. melt) the sugar and serve.

Vanilla Crème Brûlée

165 ml whipping cream	750 ml whipping cream
100 ml milk	450 ml milk
47 g sugar	210 g sugar
1 vanilla bean	4.5 vanilla beans
3 egg yolks (60 g)	13 1/2 egg yolks (270 g)
2/3 egg (37 - 41 g)	3 eggs (168 - 186 g)
3 ml vanilla extract	15 ml vanilla extract

Yield: 6 x 2 oz approx.   **Yield:** 27 x 2 oz approx.

1) Split the vanilla bean(s) in half with a knife. With the back of a knife, scrape out the vanilla pods. Put the vanilla pods and vanilla bean(s) in a pot with cream and milk. Bring cream to a rolling boil. Remove from heat. Set it aside.
2) In a mixing bowl, combine eggs (both yolks and egg(s)) and sugar. Whisk until thoroughly blended.
3) Remove the vanilla bean(s). Squeeze out as much liquid as possible back into the cream and discard the bean(s). Slowly pour and whisk the hot cream into the egg mixture. Whisk until thoroughly blended.
4) Put ramekins on a baking sheet.
5) Fill ramekins with Crème Brûlée mixture, liquid slightly below the rim.
6) Bake using the Direct Heat method, checking every 5 minutes.
7) Once the mixture is slightly solidified, remove the baking sheet from the oven. Allow ramekins to cool down at room temperature for 5 - 10 minutes and refrigerate. When Brûlée is cold, caramelize (i.e. melt) the sugar and serve.

White Chocolate Crème Brûlée

125 ml whipping cream	500 ml whipping cream
10 g sugar	40 g sugar
25 g white chocolate chips (if using chocolate chunks, chop into small pieces)	100 g white chocolate chips (if using chocolate chunks, chop into small pieces)
1 1/2 egg yolks (30 g)	6 egg yolks (120 g)
Yield: 6 x 2 oz approx.	**Yield:** 22 x 2 oz approx.

1) Put chocolate chips or pieces in a mixing bowl. Set it aside.
2) In a pot, bring cream to a rolling boil. Remove from heat. Pour hot cream over the chocolate. Whisk until chocolate is melted and blended thoroughly. Set it aside.
3) In a mixing bowl, combine eggs (both yolks and egg(s)) and sugar. Whisk until thoroughly blended.
4) Slowly pour and whisk the chocolate cream mixture into the egg mixture. Whisk until thoroughly blended.
5) Put ramekins on a baking sheet.
6) Fill ramekins with Crème Brûlée mixture, liquid slightly below the rim.
7) Bake using the Direct Heat method, checking every 5 minutes.
8) Once the mixture is slightly solidified, remove the baking sheet from the oven. Allow ramekins to cool down at room temperature for 5 - 10 minutes and refrigerate. When Brûlée is cold, caramelize (i.e. melt) the sugar and serve.

White Chocolate and Black Pepper Crème Brûlée

125 ml whipping cream	500 ml whipping cream
75 ml milk	300 ml milk
15 g sugar	60 g sugar
50 g white chocolate chips (if using chocolate chunks, chop into small pieces)	200 g white chocolate chips (if using chocolate chunks, chop into small pieces)
2 egg yolks (40 g)	8 egg yolks (160 g)
0.25 g black pepper ground	1 g black pepper ground

Yield: 6 x 2 oz approx.   **Yield:** 24 x 2 oz approx.

1) Put chocolate chips or pieces in a mixing bowl. Set it aside.
2) In a pot, bring cream and milk to a rolling boil. Remove from heat. Pour the hot cream over the chocolate. Whisk until chocolate is melted and thoroughly blended. Set it aside.
3) In a mixing bowl, combine eggs (both yolks and egg(s)), sugar and black pepper ground. Whisk until thoroughly blended.
4) Slowly pour and whisk the chocolate cream mixture into the egg mixture. Whisk until thoroughly blended.
5) Put ramekins on a baking sheet.
6) Fill ramekins with Crème Brûlée mixture, liquid slightly below the rim.
7) Bake using the Direct Heat method, checking every 5 minutes.
8) Once the mixture is slightly solidified, remove the baking sheet from the oven. Allow ramekins to cool down at room temperature for 5 - 10 minutes and refrigerate. When Brûlée is cold, caramelize (i.e. melt) the sugar and serve.

White Chocolate and Ginger Crème Brûlée

0.24 g ginger powder	1.2 g ginger powder
22 g fresh grated ginger	110 g fresh grated ginger
160 ml whipping cream	800 ml whipping cream
80 ml milk	400 ml milk
72 g white chocolate chips (if using chocolate chunks, chop into small pieces)	360 g white chocolate chips (if using chocolate chunks, chop into small pieces)
12 g sugar	60 g sugar
1 1/2 egg yolks (30 g)	8 egg yolks (160 g)
1/2 egg (28 - 31 g)	2 eggs (112 - 124 g)
Yield: 6 x 2 oz approx.	**Yield:** 30 x 2 oz approx.

The recipe below is in small quantities. Please change the amount of cream and milk required for large quantities.

1) Put chocolate chips or pieces in a mixing bowl. Set it aside.
2) In a pot, bring 160 ml cream and 80 ml milk to a rolling boil. Remove from heat. Add the sachet of fresh ginger in the hot cream and infuse for 30 minutes. (see page 40 for infusion instructions). Set it aside.
3) After the infusion time, remove the sachet and squeeze as much liquid out as possible back into the cream.
4) In a measuring cup, re-measure the cream to 240 ml. Add cream if necessary to reach 240 ml.
5) In a pot, bring the infused cream to a rolling boil. Remove from heat. Pour the hot cream into the chocolate. Whisk until chocolate is melted and thoroughly blended. Set it aside.
6) In a mixing bowl, combine eggs (both yolks and egg(s)), sugar, and ginger powder. Whisk until thoroughly blended.
7) Whisk the chocolate cream mixture into the egg mixture. Whisk until thoroughly blended.
8) Put ramekins on a baking sheet.
9) Fill ramekins with Crème Brûlée mixture, liquid slightly below the rim.
10) Bake using the Direct Heat method, checking every 5 minutes.
11) Once the mixture is slightly solidified, remove the baking sheet from the oven. Allow ramekins to cool down at room temperature for 5 - 10 minutes and refrigerate. When Brûlée is cold, caramelize (i.e. melt) the sugar and serve.

White Chocolate, Lemon, and Lavender Crème Brùlée

138 ml milk	550 ml milk
250 ml whipping cream	1000 ml whipping cream
63 g white chocolate chips (if using chocolate chunks, chop into small pieces)	250 g white chocolate chips (if using chocolate chunks, chop into small pieces)
25 g lemon zest	100 g lemon zest
0.5 g lavender flowers	2 g lavender flowers
25 g sugar	100 g sugar
3 1/4 egg yolks (65 g)	13 egg yolks (260 g)
1/2 egg (28 - 31 g)	2 eggs (112 - 124 g)
Yield: 8 x 2 oz approx.	**Yield:** 32 x 2 oz approx.

The recipe below is in small quantities. Please change the amount of cream and milk required for large quantities.

1) Put chocolate chips or pieces in a mixing bowl. Set it aside.
2) In a pot, bring 250 ml cream and 138 ml milk to a rolling boil. Remove from heat. Infuse the sachet of lavender and lemon zest in the hot cream, infuse for 30 minutes (see page 40 for infusion instructions). Set it aside.
3) After the infusion time, remove the sachet and squeeze as much liquid out as possible back into the cream.
4) In a measuring cup, re-measure the cream to 388 ml. Add cream if necessary to reach 388 ml.
5) In a pot, bring infused cream to a rolling boil. Remove from heat. Pour the hot cream into the chocolate. Whisk until chocolate is melted or thoroughly blended. Set it aside.
6) In a mixing bowl, combine eggs (both yolks and egg(s)) and sugar. Whisk until thoroughly blended.
7) Whisk the chocolate cream mixture into the egg mixture. Whisk until thoroughly blended.
8) Put ramekins on a baking sheet.
9) Fill ramekins with Crème Brûlée mixture, liquid slightly below the rim.
10) Bake using the Direct Heat method, checking every 5 minutes.
11) Once the mixture is slightly solidified, remove the baking sheet from the oven. Allow ramekins to cool down at room temperature for 5 - 10 minutes and refrigerate. When Brûlée is cold, caramelize (i.e. melt) the sugar and serve.

Yam and Vanilla Bean Crème Brûlée

125 g roasted yam (175 - 200 g) fresh yam, roasted in the oven at 400°F (205°C) until tender)	500 g roasted yam (700 - 800 g) fresh yam, roasted in the oven at 400°F (205°C) until tender)
250 ml whipping cream	1000 ml whipping cream
50 g sugar	100 g sugar
1 vanilla bean	4 vanilla beans
1 1/2 egg yolks (30 g)	6 egg yolks (120 g)
1/2 egg (28 - 31 g)	2 eggs (112 - 124 g)
1 ml vanilla extract	4 ml vanilla extract

Yield: 8 x 2 oz approx.   **Yield:** 32 x 2 oz approx.

The recipe below is in small quantities. Please change the amount of cream and milk required for large quantities.

1) Preheat oven to 400°F (205°C). Roast the yam (175 - 200 g) in the oven with skin on until yam is tender (pierce through with a fork). Approx. 1 hour. Rest to cool down.
2) In a food processor or blender, purée 125 g of roasted yam with 125 ml whipping cream until smooth. Set it aside.
3) Split the vanilla bean(s) in half with a knife. With the back of a knife, scrape out the vanilla pods. Put the vanilla pods and vanilla bean(s) in a pot with the rest of the cream (125 ml). Bring the cream to a rolling boil. Remove from heat. Set it aside.
4) In a mixing bowl, combine eggs (both yolks and egg(s)) and sugar. Whisk until thoroughly blended.
5) Slowly pour and whisk the hot cream into the egg mixture. Whisk until thoroughly blended. Remove the vanilla bean(s) and squeeze as much liquid out as possible back into the cream. Discard the vanilla bean(s)
6) Whisk the yam purée into the cream mixture.
7) Put ramekins on a baking sheet.
8) Fill ramekins with Crème Brûlée mixture, liquid slightly below the rim.
9) Bake using the Direct Heat method, checking every 5 minutes.
10) Once the mixture is slightly solidified, remove the baking sheet from the oven. Allow ramekins to cool down at room temperature for 5 - 10 minutes and refrigerate. When Brûlée is cold, caramelize (i.e. melt) the sugar and serve.

INDEX

Almond & white chocolate Crème Brûlée	p.54
Avocado Crème Brûlée	p.55
Baking	p.42
Banana & passion fruit Crème Brûlée	p.56
Baking sheets	p.18
Basil & lemon Crème Brûlée	p.57
Beet Crème Brûlée	p.58
Blow torch	p.19
Blueberry & butter Crème Brûlée	p.59
Bowls	p.17
Caramel apple Crème Brûlée	p.60
Caramel candy Crème Brûlée	p.61
Carrot & cumin Crème Brûlée	p.62
Ceramic bowls	p.18
Chocolate & chili Crème Brûlée	p.63
Chocolate chip cookie Crème Brûlée	p.64
Chocolate & mint Crème Brûlée	p.65
Chocolate & orange Crème Brûlée	p.66
Chocolate & raspberry Crème Brûlée	p.67
Chokecherry Crème Brûlée	p.68
Cinnamon & maple syrup Crème Brûlée	p.69
Coconut Crème Brûlée	p.70
Coconut & vanilla Crème Brûlée	p.71
Cranberry Crème Brûlée	p.72

Cream...	p.20
Dragon fruit Crème Brûlée............................	p.73
Earl Grey tea Crème Brûlée.........................	p.74
Eggs...	p.32
Egg composition...	p.33
Egg grading..	p.35
Eggnog Crème Brûlée..................................	p.75
Egg sizing...	p.35
Egg shell..	p.32
Egg white...	p.33
Egg yolk...	p.33
Espresso Crème Brûlée...............................	p.76
Example of Direct Heat method..................	p.47
Fig Crème Brûlée..	p.77
Fireball whisky Crème Brûlée......................	p.78
Foie gras & black truffle Crème Brûlée........	p.79
Foie gras torchon..	p.80
Garlic & thyme Crème Brûlée......................	p.81
Gooseberry Crème Brûlée...........................	p.82
Green apple and brandy Crème Brûlée........	p.83
Honey & dill Crème Brûlée..........................	p.84
Ice bath..	p.42
Infusion..	p.40
Ingredients...	p.20

Introduction	p.12
Kahlua Crème Brûlée	p.85
Lavender Crème Brûlée	p.86
Lemon & chardonnay wine Crème Brûlée	p.87
Lemon, vanilla & cinnamon Crème Brûlée	p.88
Maple wine Crème Brûlée	p.98
Materials	p.15
Measuring tools	p.17
Milk composition	p.25
Milk varieties	p.25
Mochaccino Crème Brûlée	p.99
Orange & ginger Crème Brûlée	p.100
Other equipment	p.19
Praline Crème Brûlée	p.101
Pumpkin Crème Brûlée	p.102
Ramekins	p.18
Reeses peanut butter cup Crème Brûlée	p.103
Recipes	p.53
Rolo Crème Brûlée	p.104
Rosemary Crème Brûlée	p.105
Saffron & honey Crème Brûlée	p.106
Strawberry & soya bean Crème Brûlée	p.107
Strawberry & vanilla Crème Brûlée	p.108
Step by step Bain Marie method	p.45

Step by step Direct Heat method............................	p.46
Sugar..	p.28
Sugar extraction...	p.29
Sugar varieties...	p.30
Techniques...	p.39
Toaster ovens...	p.19
Vanilla Crème Brûlée...	p.109
Weights..	p.17
Whisk...	p.16
Whisking...	p.40
White chocolate Crème Brûlée...............................	p.110
White chocolate & black pepper Crème Brûlée.......	p.111
White chocolate & ginger Crème Brûlée.................	p.112
White chocolate, lemon & lavender Crème Brûlée..	p.113
Yam & vanilla Crème Brûlée.................................	p.114

References

Introduction

[1] *The Oxford Companion to Sugar and Sweets*. Oxford University Press. 1 April 2015. pp. 383–. ISBN 978-0-19-931362-4.
[2] https://en.wikipedia.org/wiki/Cr%C3%A8me_br%C3%BB%C3%A9e#History
[3] https://www.trin.cam.ac.uk/about/historical-overview/trinity-burnt-cream/
[4 & 5] http://gourmet.lovetoknow.com/Creme_Brulee_History

Cream

[6] came from many resources listed below
[7] https://en.wikipedia.org/wiki/Cream
The Professional Pastry Chef, 3rd edition, Bo Friberg, Van Nostrand Reinhold. 1996. pp. 1093-1094. ISBN # 0-442-01597-6
The Science of Good Food, David Joachim and Andrew Scholoss with A. Philip Handel, Ph.D. Robert Rose 2008, Pp. 399-404, ISBN # 123456789TCP161514131211100908
Wellness Foods A to Z, Sheldon Margen, M.D. Health Letter Associates 2002, Pp. 393-402. ISBN#0-929661-70-2
The New Professional Chef, 6 edition, The Culinary Institute of America. Van Nostrand Reinhold. 1996. pp. 150-152. ISBN # 0-442-01961-0
Joy of Cooking, Irma S. Rombauer, Marion Rombauer Becker and Ethan Becker, Simon & Schuster Inc. 1997, pp. 1070-1071, ISBN#0-684-81870-1
https://apps.fas.usda.gov/psdonline/circulars/dairy.pdf
http://www.dairyinfo.gc.ca/index_e.php?s1=dff-fcil&s2=cons&s3=consglo&s4=tm-lt
http://water.usgs.gov/edu/propertyyou.html
Wellness Foods A to Z, Sheldon Margen, M.D. Health Letter Associates, 2002. Pp. 395. ISBN#0-929661-70-2

Egg

[19] Information came from many resources listed below
[20] The New Professional Chef, 6 edition, The Culinary Institute of America. Van Nostrand Reinhold. 1996. pp. 156-158. ISBN # 0-442-01961-0
[21]The Science of Good Food, David Joachim and Andrew Scholoss with A. Philip Handel, Ph.D. Robert Rose 2008, Pp. 204, ISBN # 123456789TCP161514131211100908
The Professional Pastry Chef, 3rd edition, Bo Friberg, Van Nostrand Reinhold. 1996. pp. 1094-1095 ISBN # 0-442-01597-6
The Science of Good Food, David Joachim and Andrew Scholoss with A. Philip Handel, Ph.D. Robert Rose 2008, Pp. 201-206, ISBN? 123456789TCP161514131211100908
Wellness Foods A to Z, Sheldon Margen, M.D. Health Letter Associates 2002, Pp. 279-281. ISBN#0-929661-70-2
Joy of Cooking, Irma S. Rombauer, Marion Rombauer Becker and Ethan Becker, Simon & Schuster Inc. 1997, pp. 121-123, ISBN#0-684-81870-1
The New Larousse Gastronomique, Prosper Montagné, Crown Publishers, INC. New York 1978, pp. 334-335, ISBN#0-517-53137-2
The World Book Encyclopedia, E volume 6, A Scott Fetzer company Chicago, 2016, pp. 116-118, ISBN#978-0-7166-0116-6

Egg Chemistry [22]

https://www.giapo.com/the-chemistry-of-egg-whites/
https://www.exploratorium.edu/cooking/icooks/article_5-03.html
https://www.exploratorium.edu/cooking/eggs/eggscience.html
http://www.thekitchn.com/baking-school-day-1-all-about-eggs-and-baking-222479
https://en.wikipedia.org/wiki/Egg_white
https://en.wikipedia.org/wiki/Emulsion

Milk

[8 & 15] came from many resources listed below
[9 & 10] https://apps.fas.usda.gov/psdonline/circulars/dairy.pdf
http://www.milkunleashed.com/shelf-safe-milk/aseptic-packaging-uht-milk.html
[11] http://www.dairyinfo.gc.ca/index_e.php?s1=dff-fcil&s2=cons&s3=consglo&s4=tm-lt
[12] http://water.usgs.gov/edu/propertyyou.html
[13] Wellness Foods A to Z, Sheldon Margen, M.D. Health Letter Associates, 2002. Pp. 395. ISBN#0-929661-70-2
[14] https://en.wikipedia.org/wiki/Milk
https://www.dairygoodness.ca/milk
http://milk.procon.org/view.timeline.php?timelineID=000018
http://www.microbecolhealthdis.net/index.php/mehd/article/viewFile/7606/8940
https://bcdairy.ca/milk/articles/the-probiotic-effects-of-lactic-acid-bacteria
The New Professional Chef, 6 edition, The Culinary Institute of America. Van Nostrand Reinhold. 1996. pp. 150-152. ISBN # 0-442-01961-0
The Professional Pastry Chef, 3rd edition, Bo Friberg, Van Nostrand Reinhold. 1996. pp. 1093-1094. ISBN # 0-442-01597-6
The Science of Good Food, David Joachim and Andrew Scholoss with A. Philip Handel, Ph.D. Robert Rose 2008, Pp. 399-404, ISBN? 123456789TCP161514131211100908
Wellness Foods A to Z, Sheldon Margen, M.D. Health Letter Associates 2002, Pp. 393-402. ISBN#0-929661-70-2
Joy of Cooking, Irma S. Rombauer, Marion Rombauer Becker and Ethan Becker, Simon & Schuster Inc. 1997, pp. 1069-1070, ISBN#0-684-81870-1
The New Larousse Gastronomique, Prosper Montagné, Crown Publishers, INC. New York 1978, pp. 589-590, ISBN#0-517-53137-2
The World Book Encyclopedia, M volume 13, A Scott Fetzer company Chicago, 2016, pp. 545-550, ISBN#978-0-7166-0116-6

Sugar

[16] came from many resources listed below
[17] https://apps.fas.usda.gov/psdonline/circulars/Sugar.pdf
[18] http://www.sugar.ca/Nutrition-Information-Service/Consumers/How-Much-Sugar-Do-Canadians-Eat.aspx
https://apps.fas.usda.gov/psdonline/circulars/Sugar.pdf
http://www.macleans.ca/society/health/sugar-and-health-how-much-sugar-do-you-eat-in-a-year/

Sugar

The Professional Pastry Chef, 3rd edition, Bo Friberg, Van Nostrand Reinhold. 1996. pp. 928 – 933, pp. 1114-1115. ISBN # 0-442-01597-6

The Science of Good Food, David Joachim and Andrew Scholoss with A. Philip Handel, Ph.D. Robert Rose 2008, Pp. 551-555, ISBN? 123456789TCP1615141312111100908

Wellness Foods A to Z, Sheldon Margen, M.D. Health Letter Associates 2002, Pp. 560-564. ISBN#0-929661-70-2

The New Professional Chef, 6 edition, The Culinary Institute of America. Van Nostrand Reinhold. 1996. pp. 174. ISBN # 0-442-01961-0

The New Larousse Gastronomique, Prosper Montagné, Crown Publishers, INC. New York 1978, pp. 905-908, ISBN#0-517-53137-2

https://www.sugar.org/all-about-sugar/types-of-sugar/

https://en.wikipedia.org/wiki/Sugar

http://www.sugar.ca/Nutrition-Information-Service/Consumers/About-Sugar/Types-of-Sugar.aspx

http://www.thekitchn.com/a-complete-visual-guide-to-sugar-ingredient-intelligence-213715

The World Book Encyclopedia, S volume 18, A Scott Fetzer company Chicago, 2016, pp. 959-963, ISBN#978-0-7166-0116-6

Ice Bath

[23] http://rouxbe.com/tips-techniques/276-what-is-an-ice-bath
http://www.thekitchn.com/food-safety-ice-baths-48957

[24] The Sanitation Code for Canada's Foodservice Indsutry - Canadain Restaurant Association, 1991

about the author

Cam Tran began his culinary arts career in 1993 working as an assistant alongside a Red Seal chef. Since then, his interests in cooking has led him to understand the concept of Western cuisine far beyond the traditional Chinese dishes he learned from his father. Under the apprenticeship of Ono Sadao, the chef and owner of Edohei Japanese Restaurant in Winnipeg, Manitoba, Canada, Cam was elevated to First Cook while completing his diploma from Gordon Bell High School. In 1999, Chef Tran received his Culinary Arts diploma from Red River College, graduating with honours. In 2002, having spent four years working at a five-star French restaurant, La Vieille Gare, he entered the medical field working as a health care assistant while he designed wedding cakes for clients on his spare time.

Chef Tran returned to his passion for culinary arts in 2011 having enrolled at the Gastronomicom International Culinary Art School in Agde, France, where he graduated with a diploma in pastry. Having trained under Florent Cantaut, a Two-Michelin star chef, he worked as the assistant pastry chef for two hotels, Hotel l'Astragale and Hotel Mandarin; and one restaurant, La Bouillabaisse. Within a month of beginning his pastry apprenticeship, Chef Tran was appointed the Head Pastry Chef for Hotel Mandarin, Saint-Tropez.

After his studies in France, Cam Tran travelled extensively through Vietnam and China while expanding his knowledge in Asian cuisine. In 2012, he returned to Winnipeg to open up his own establishment, Café Ce Soir.

CPSIA information can be obtained at www.ICGtesting.com
Printed in the USA
BVIW120355251118
533693BV00003B/3